The

The Prevalent Forms c

HOUGHTON MIFFLIN COMPANY · BOSTON

NEW YORK ATLANTA GENEVA, ILL. DALLAS PALO ALTO

THE POPULAR ARTICLE

THE PROFESSIONAL ARTICLE

rose THE PERSONAL ESSAY

THE FORMAL ESSAY

THE CRITICAL REVIEW

Otis Winchester · Winston Weathers

THE UNIVERSITY OF TULSA, OKLAHOMA

PRINTED IN THE U.S.A.

TO THE STUDENT

THIS IS A BOOK for the college writer who wants to understand the prose forms he reads in magazines and journals by writing them himself, for the student who wants to begin looking beyond the university classroom to the larger world of letters.

Until now your writing experience has probably been limited to themes and compositions and research papers. These forms are at best academic exercises, artificial and unrealistic because they are nothing like what you will be reading and, perhaps, writing in the course of your active career. At worst they are such indefinite forms that they are not even reasonable exercises. To ask you to prepare a piece of writing for which there are no traditions or even examples in literature is to expect more of you, a student writer, than any editor would dare of a professional. In any case, surely you have written exercises long enough and are now ready to begin using those forms you must use if you are to be read seriously — the popular article, the professional article, the personal essay, the formal essay, and the critical review.

OTIS WINCHESTER
WINSTON WEATHERS

Tulsa, Oklahoma

CONTENTS

1

The Necessity of Form

To write well you must know your form — its purposes, characteristics, and traditions. Moreover, if you want to be read, you must master those forms used by publishing writers to express their thoughts in journals and magazines. Of course, you may not have literary ambitions at all, or you may never get beyond the stage of idly contemplating the prospect. But even if you have no immediate desire to publish, you will undoubtedly read more articles, essays, and reviews than other prose; and the best way to learn the intricacies of these prevalent forms of prose is to try your hand at writing them. The most prevalent forms today are the popular article, the professional article, the personal essay, the formal essay, and the critical review.

A Sense of Form

A sense of form involves more than knowing how to manage certain genres, more than knowing the rules and regulations of language. Important as it is for the writer, a sense of form is difficult to define. It has its beginnings in the knowledge and the respect of good writing and literary tradition, which in time leads to judgment and taste, and finally becomes a wholeness of vision that enables the writer to shape his prose toward some preconsidered design in the confidence that the finished piece of writing will be as he imagined.

For whom you are writing and what you are writing about influences the shape of your prose as much as the forms you use. But since readers appreciate a variety of reading fare and since the same subject can be treated in a variety of ways, form is likely to be the main consideration. The various prose forms impose decidedly different patterns on not only the final product but on your whole approach. As soon as you decide on a form — the popular or scholarly article, the personal or formal essay, the critical review — you make a commitment. You will follow pretty much the same steps in the writing process as other writers; you will work within a rather definite and sometimes elaborate framework; and you will produce something that is in many ways like others of its kind.

Each of the prevalent forms described here has proven particularly convenient and expressive in the context for which it was designed, or it would be quickly discarded for something better. Though all are relatively modern, each is the product of a long evolution at the hands of publishing writers, many of them great stylists; and each continues to be modified to suit a changing society. For these are pragmatic forms, each providing a special kind of comment on the human condition in a technological age, yet each retaining that heightened vision and language which is the *sine qua non* of literature.

Form, in the sense we have been using the term here, involves much of what is considered in the definition or description of a genre: its length, purpose, degree of formality. (Clearly each genre possesses qualities that distinguish it from others.) In some cases, however, form is imposed more by the writer and by the content and meaning of the work than by those more obvious and objective qualities of genre. The writer's style is a personal and infinitely variable source of form. And so is content, for most subjects have an inherent form that is almost always reflected in the form of a literary work. Form is a product of those qualities which identify a work as being of a particular genre, which grow naturally out of the content and meaning to give it pattern, and which are imposed by the writer's style to shape his materials — everything, in short, that contributes to a work's unity.

Still, form is commonly misunderstood. The less-experienced writer is apt to think of it as a positive hindrance to spontaneous self-expression. Yet he most of all is likely to be frustrated by his own inarticulateness — the very thing a sense of form would remedy. For it is a "formula," a recipe containing the basic ingredients and giving directions for making an effective statement. What appears to be a rejection of form can, in fact, be no more than a search for new forms; and a search for new forms leads, ironically for the writer who supposed he could do without it, to a preoccupation with form. An ignorance of form leads to a contempt for form. We all know "poets" who look embarrassingly blank at the mention of "ode" or "iambic pentameter" but who hotly defend the superiority of their peculiarly irregular (and unread) verse. The prose writer who tries to practice his art without knowing anything of its form is no less a dilettante. A sense of form, unless it is carried to neo-classical extremes (which is highly unlikely in mid-twentieth-century America), is a necessity for good writing.

Let us review briefly certain commonplaces of form: Everything you write should possess *clarity and effectiveness.* To achieve this you must follow a rather definite *writing process.* And what you ultimately want is a *readable manuscript.*

Clarity and Effectiveness

The immediate objects of form are clarity and effectiveness. You cannot be understood, much less be forceful or impressive, if you prefer ambiguities, labyrinthine constructions, and awkward vocabulary over clean and unclouded words; at its best, effective form will lead to an aesthetic experience, not a mere pedestrian statement.

Clarity

In striving for clarity you will want to master those aspects of form that contribute most immediately to intelligible communication. To achieve clarity, you must be able to control the elements of your article, essay, or review by putting them in order; connecting them, one with another; emphasizing certain parts, subordinating others; and elaborating upon those parts that need greater illustration and demonstration.

Even the simplest pieces of writing have parts and divisions. Most are actually a complex of smaller individual messages, thoughts, ideas that are being mustered together to make up the larger statement that you are passing on to a reader.

Let us suppose that out of a haze of sensations, emotions, vague thoughts and ideas, you have been able to put together the beginnings of an announcement addressed to your fellow students to be published in the campus newspaper:

1. I want you to meet with us tonight.
2. We are going to discuss the new freshman reading list.
3. Several of us think the list is too long.
4. We think the list contains too few modern European authors.
5. John Whitcomb and I have organized a meeting.
6. We will meet in the Student Union at seven-thirty.
7. Many of you have expressed an interest in the reading list.
8. John Whitcomb and I believe the student body should make some intelligent statement about the reading list.

Obviously it is in no shape to print in the paper yet.

Your first job in order to achieve the wanted clarity is to organize your accumulated thoughts into a single, coherent message. Which of the above eight thoughts will you mention first, which second, which third? Assuming that each statement is clear in itself, you have the writing objective of making clarity out of the whole. You decide, first, that the notice will make a little more sense if you *order* your thoughts:

> Several of us think the freshman reading list is too long. We think the list contains too few modern European authors. John Whitcomb and I believe the student body should make some intelligent statement about the reading list. We are going to discuss the new freshman reading list tonight. John and I have organized the meeting. We will meet in the Student

Union at seven-thirty. Many of you have expressed an interest in the reading list. I want you to meet with us tonight.

Your fellow students will be able to follow your thoughts — yet they will get more out of your announcement if you will somehow *connect* the parts. The way they are now, they have a blunt, disconnected quality to them. The thoughts are all there, but they are not tied together into a single message. Also, you may wish to make some of your words more definite, more precise. Perhaps you can try something like this:

Several of us think the freshman reading list is too long, *and* we think the list contains too few modern European authors. John Whitcomb and I, *among others,* believe *responsible students* should make some intelligent statement about the reading list *to the faculty. Therefore, a number of us* are going to discuss the new freshman reading list, *and* John and I have organized a meeting *for that purpose.* We will meet in the Student Union at seven-thirty. *Since* many of you have expressed an interest in the reading list, I want you to meet with us tonight.

Your fellow students, in all likelihood, are beginning to listen to what you have to say now and to understand your words better. Perhaps you can clarify the picture even more, if in addition to the *ordering* and *connecting* that you have already done, you now give some attention to *emphasis* and *subordination.*

Agreeing with those who think the freshman reading list is too long and contains too few modern European authors, John Whitcomb and I, among others, believe that — as responsible students — we should make some intelligent statement about the list to the faculty. Therefore, a number of us are going to discuss the list tonight, *at seven-thirty, in the Student Union, at a meeting organized by John and me for that purpose.* Since many of you have expressed an interest in the reading list, I want you to meet with us.

With this version, you have not only ordered and connected your thoughts, but you have played up the main thoughts — a statement to the faculty should be made, a meeting is to be held to prepare such a statement, and students should attend. Not wishing to go into a detailed discussion of what is wrong with the list, you have subordinated your criticisms. The announcement is in much better shape now than it was when you first began. The only thing left to do, really, is to *elaborate* a bit on the individual thoughts so as to make the announcement more substantial and meaningful.

> Agreeing with those who think the freshman reading list is too long and contains too few modern European authors, John Whitcomb, *freshman class president,* and I believe that we should make, *as seriously concerned members of the University* community, some intelligent statement about the list to the *English Department* faculty. Therefore for that purpose, a number of us *who have examined the list carefully and have talked privately with some of our professors,* are going to discuss the list tonight, at seven-thirty, in the Student Union, at a meeting that John and I have organized. Since many of you have expressed an interest in the reading list, I want you to meet with us.

By means of order, connections, emphasis and subordination, and elaboration, you have come up with a clear statement. You will see that by giving your attention to a few simple matters you can greatly improve the form of your writing.

Effectiveness

Yet many a writer who manages to express himself with mathematical precision and well-engineered directness has found himself failing to make contact with those around him. People understand what he is saying — his clarity is sometimes rather magnificent — but their understanding results in no response, in no intellectual or emotional return. To make your writing not only reach your readers but stick tight and hold firm you must strive not only to write clearly, but also to write effectively.

If you rush to your neighbor and cry out, "Mr. Muggleridge just went mad and set fire to your garage and is threatening your wife with an ax!" you need not have any neighborly concern with diction, sentence structure, emphasis, or rhetorical texture in order to get the message across. But if your reader is not immediately or deeply concerned, you may coax him into swallowing it nevertheless by putting honey on the edge of the cup. Because in language you can create patterns and arrangements, because you can take advantage of the sensory aspect and connotative aura of words, you can create for readers a number of pleasurable experiences distinguished from actual meaning but contributing to real communication.

To write well, you must be able to maintain word interest within your messages, maintain an interesting variety of sentence and paragraph construction, maintain rhetorical interest. You must, in other words, use your full repertoire of stylistic fireworks to stun your reader to wakefulness and tantalize his slumbering senses.

Let us suppose you want to say something serious about the disillusioned generation following World War II, something about the failure of cultural adjustments after the holocaust of the war and the bomb. You will, of course, have to construct your message with order, connection, emphasis, and elaboration — but you will also have to give attention to effectiveness:

> After the war, we wasted our lives in weary pastimes that brought us no rewards, no victories, no satisfaction, but left us lost in dark forests of our own sad making.

Even if your reader is not immediately interested in your subject, you have given him, in the first sentence of your message, the opportunity to respond to certain language experiences — the alliteration of the w's, s's, l's; the three parallel direct objects — "no rewards, no victories, no satisfaction"; the metaphor in the conclusion. And as you continue with the message, you will continue giving your reader this sort of language experience.

> Weary with the labor of the battlefield, we avoided the labor of peace. We fled toward frolic. We fled toward all

> the delicious sensations we had missed. We fled toward all the pleasures and trivialities we had so long been denied and to which we knew we were entitled. But our running brought us nowhere. On the other side of every frivolous escape from reality sat the dark truth, waiting and biding its time.

Here you have continued the alliteration of the w's; you have deliberately increased the length of each succeeding sentence in the series beginning "We fled . . ." in order to relieve any possible monotony and also to set up the sentence that follows, "But our running brought us nowhere," which in its relative shortness seems to stand out.

> So where to go? No place at all. So what to do? Nothing whatsoever. Put away the toys. Turn off the music. We could no longer pretend the dark forest was a kingdom of light.

In this brief paragraph, you have deliberately created an exceptional paragraph pattern to contrast with the more normal paragraphs preceding and following. This brief paragraph, essentially transitional, has been set off from the other paragraphs not only in shortness, but with an essentially elliptical sentence style.

> After the war, we came home disillusioned and thought we could forget the horrors of the past and ignore the problems of the present. But soon we learned that life's battles are never over. Only the nature of the belligerency changes. And since we must fight, we chose to fight in the open, rather than in the dark places we had created out of our own intellectual and moral blindness.

By giving attention in this message to word choice, to sound patterns, to sentence structures, to paragraph structures, to metaphors and other figures, you have communicated with your reader not only with clarity but with effectiveness as well.

In your study of writing, you will learn that by vocabulary, rhetorical, and structural enrichment, you will increase the general readability of your prose. Indeed, a sense of form involves not only writing correctly and clearly, but making your writing intriguing, stimulating, aesthetically satisfying.

The Writing Process

The best habit any writer can develop, as he strives for clarity and effectiveness within form, is rewriting. While the thought you give to your material before you actually begin putting words on paper is important, most of your writing effort will be concentrated on reshaping and revising those words once they are down. With experience you will learn which writing methods work best for you. Many of these creative habits will be distinctive—you may discover that you write best on Sunday afternoons with the blinds drawn while listening to Wagner. But we can safely generalize about some parts of the writing process, at least about the program most publishing writers seem more or less to follow.

Jottings

Jot down some preliminary notes for your article, essay, or review. A list of main thoughts in about the order you expect to take them up is a good place to begin. You may have been putting down ideas over a period of time, just as they came to you. (No serious writer is ever without a note pad or some cards carried just for this purpose.) Sooner or later you must begin putting something down on paper, and you will write more fluently if these tentative efforts are jottings rather than a first draft or even an outline. If what you are writing is rather short and casual, such as a personal essay, and if you are reasonably familiar with your subject and a fairly confident writer, you may be able to make a first draft without further preliminaries. However, if you are writing something like a scholarly article or formal essay, you will probably need more of a synopsis or outline.

The Outline

Most writers find that their work goes more smoothly if they use some kind of outline, generally one of these three: If your jottings are rather complete and orderly, they may already constitute a *preliminary* or *inventory outline.* But since it is easier to plan a short work in terms of topics scaled to paragraph size, you may find the *paragraph outline* even more useful. For a longer work on a difficult subject you may prefer the *noun-phrase* or *sentence outline,* one that is so detailed the writer need only flesh out the discussion and add transitions to have a first draft.

Remember this, however: you can over-plan almost as easily as you can under-plan. Jottings and outlines are useful because your materials can be more easily rephrased, juggled, or discarded at this stage than later. Do not let these pre-writing gestures freeze your conceptions too soon; retain as much flexibility as possible not only in these early stages of writing but even through the final draft.

The Rough Draft

In this first draft establish the general shape and accumulate most of the materials that will make up your work. Concentrate on the subject and thesis and overall unity, letting the finer points go until later. There is much to be said for writing as much as you can as rapidly as you can at this point, getting the materials down so you will have something to work with later, attaining a momentum that may lead you to write more knowledgeably and fluently than you supposed yourself capable.

The Controlled Draft

In this second draft you can begin trimming down, tightening up what you wrote earlier. Eliminate, expand, rearrange, rephrase. Especially consider proportion, emphasis, sentence and paragraph structure, and diction. Try to shape this draft toward the form the final work is to take.

The Polished Draft

In this third draft clear up whatever problems remain. The general readability of your prose can often be greatly improved by a few final touches. And the accuracy of spelling, punctuation, and grammar needs to be checked.

The Cold Reading

Put what you have written aside for at least twenty-four hours. Then give it a final critical reading. Remember that the reader has only these words; what they do not tell him of your thinking on this subject he will never know.

The Finished Manuscript

All that remains now is to prepare a final copy of the article, essay, or review — carefully proofreading to be sure it is absolutely neat and correct. Your reader will do the rest.

The Readable Manuscript

With the completion of the finished manuscript your work is done; the manuscript is quite literally out of your hands; and no explanation or apologies can have any effect on its reception. The handing over of your manuscript to a reader is a kind of symbolic gesture. You imply that the subject has been treated knowledgeably and fairly, that the art of the personal essay (or whatever the form) has been upheld, that the reader will find something significant and accessible, and that you have written your best — in short, that you have created something of publishable quality.

And attention to some final details will do much to insure your manuscript a considerate reading. Many of these final details have to do with what will be for your reader's first impressions, the physical appearance of the manuscript. Paradoxically, you don't want your reader to notice the typewritten page at all. You want him to look through the page to what thoughts and visions lie beyond. And the best way to avoid misdirecting his attention is to be utterly correct, neat, and conventional.

Paper

Always use white, standard size (8½ x 11), medium weight (16 or 20 pound) bond (25% cotton fibre is ideal). Do not use any of the so-called erasable papers, for their tendency to smear is such that you cannot have a neat page for very long. And do not use onion skin except for carbons for your own files.

Typing

A typewriter is the best investment a college writer can make and is absolutely essential if you expect to write for publication. The portable electrics are good and cost little more than many portable standards. Except for the inconvenience, an office typewriter is often a good buy — it will always give you better copy than a standard portable. The conventional pica or elite is safest, but some of the less radical newer type faces are acceptable. Script style type, however, is definitely out. Use a nylon or possibly silk ribbon, not cotton. An all black ribbon is a better buy than a red and black one since you can turn it over to get twice the life. But don't use any ribbon so long that the type becomes illegible.

Margins, Spacing, Page Numbering, Identification

Margins on the first page should be two inches above the title, four spaces below, with the title centered. Margins on subsequent pages should be one and one-half inches at the top and on the left side, one inch at the right and bottom. Indent five to seven spaces for paragraphs. Double space, except for prose quotes running to two or more lines; these should be indented approximately one inch more and single spaced. (On earlier drafts you may want to triple space, leaving yourself more room for revisions.) All pages after the first should be numbered with Arabic numerals (2, 3, 4, etc.) in the upper right-hand corner. Your name plus address or other information requested by the instructor should appear in the upper left-hand corner of the first page.

Proofing and Correcting

Your final proofreading must be the most critical and careful of all because it is the last. Any manuscript submitted to an editor or instructor must be neat and error free. To get it this way you may need to retype certain pages or even the entire manuscript. Minor errors — spelling, punctuation, and typographical bloopers — can sometimes be corrected by a neat erasure followed by retyping. (The white carbon paper made for this purpose works pretty well, but once the page is out of the machine you really have to erase.) More serious errors require more drastic measures. To delete, draw a line horizontally through the words. To add, there or elsewhere, print (or type) the correction above and place a caret (‸) below the line. Other proofreader's marks are often useful: ¶ (paragraph), no ¶ (no paragraph), ∽ (reverse these letters, words), > (vertical space), ∧ (horizontal space). Corrections on the final manuscript, even obvious ones, are not damning if they are few, neat, and clear. Errors, no matter how neat the copy, are still errors.

Some Additional Good Advice

Keep a copy, preferably a carbon with final corrections written in, of everything you write. Don't even be too quick to throw away early drafts and working notes. Build a library of writer's reference books: at the very least you should own a really good dictionary, a thesaurus, a book on usage like Fowler's *Modern English Usage* (Oxford), and if you are an unsteady speller, Leslie's *20,000 Words* (McGraw-Hill).

2

The Popular Article

The article, a factual discussion of from several hundred to several thousand words on a fairly definite subject, is written to satisfy a practical reader in a utilitarian age. Informative rather than speculative, the article offers explanations and proofs rather than reflections and conjectures. It is written communication of the most direct and literal kind, avoiding the subtle, the suggestive, and the exquisite. The writer is an authority rather than a personality. In view of its impersonal preoccupation with subject and matter-of-fact idiom, the article can hardly be considered "literary." But this does not detract from the specific kind of skill required to write the article or, certainly, from the favor it has found with the reading public. Still, the term "article" is so commonly misused that we must remind ourselves it is a distinct form — more objective than the essay, less expressive of opinion than the editorial, and written in greater depth than the news story.

We cannot generalize about the article for very long without making a distinction between the *popular* and the *professional* article. The popular articles in magazines and newspapers are more likely to deal with subjects their numerous readers will find timely if not sensational and in a way that is rather more spritely than thorough. The scholarly or serious articles found in learned and professional journals are almost always the specialized, detailed, and closely reasoned treatments their somewhat more knowledgeable readers expect.

The Popular Article as a Form

A more detailed description of the popular article must take up these topics: the accommodation of a subject to a class of readers, the selection and arrangement of details on the basis of interest, and the employment of a highly readable, journalistic style.

The accommodation of a subject to a class of readers is clearly the principal object of the popular article. You begin with a subject — but quickly look ahead to the reader. Not only is the choice of subjects influenced by the reader's preoccupations and psychology, but so is the way in which any subject is developed. For the subject, if not immediately attractive, must be quickly made so; you first find a relevant subject and then make it more relevant. The popular article is instructive, even persuasive, exploring those subjects which have something to do with "living the good life." But at the same time it brings pleasure to a reader who enjoys indulging his curiosity. So you go looking for subjects, equipped with a fair knowledge of your reading audience and your subject. And most of your writing effort will be devoted to bringing this subject and this reader together.

Your subjects will invariably be the significant, the striking, the anecdotal, the inherently interesting (anything, in short, that appeals to those human hopes and fears which are the common lot and by so doing excites humor, pathos, fear, romance, and above all curiosity). And your reader will just as surely be one who through the article would become a part of the scheme of things (for not knowing is not belonging) and more affluent (for knowledge of the world remains the principal way of knowing and attaining our heart's desires). The article's greatest appeal is to that vast middle class of which we are virtually all members. Earnest, hard-working, eager to learn and succeed, we are fascinated by the odd and unusual, but especially attracted by the familiar and useful—people, places, new ideas, how-to-do-it pieces, exposés, personal experiences. A run-down of recently published titles reveals a great deal about both the subjects and readers of popular articles: "G. H. Hardy: The Pure Mathematician" (C. P. Snow, *Atlantic*), "Cast Iron Furniture" (John Mebane, *Better Homes and Gardens*), "The Dawn, the Totem, the Drums: African Literature in the Grip of Harsh Realities" (Wilfred Cartey, *Commonweal*), "Dr. von Braun's All-Purpose Space Machine" (Gene Bylinsky, *Fortune*), "Gibraltar" (Anthony Burgess, *Holiday*), "Coming to Terms with the New Art" (Emily Genauer, *House Beautiful*), "Should This Sex Research Be Allowed to Go On?" (Lois Chevaliar, *Ladies' Home Journal*), "When an American Negro Returns to Africa" (Ernest Dunham, *Look*), "Young Marriage: What Happens When Parents Pay the Bills" (Samuel Grafton, *McCall's*), "College President: Salesman, Philosopher, Riot Preventer" (Andrew Hacker, *The New York Times Magazine*), "Big Fly: Big Trout" (V. C. Marinaro, *Outdoor Life*), "Change in Mixed Marriages" (J. C. Wynn, *Presbyterian Life*), "Better Coed Than Dead" (*Time*), "Medicare: Headache or Cure-all?" (Steven M. Spencer, *The Saturday Evening Post*).

In a form which would make the most of an arresting subject and a fascinated reader, *the selection and arrangement of details on the basis of reader interest* follows naturally. The popular article tells the reader all he wants to know and needs to know for his immediate purposes about the subject, but does not bore him with too many or with unessential details. And the popular article relies upon the most lively sort of details: anecdotes, quotations, examples, analogies, metaphors, similes, active descriptions, animated narratives. Extensive use of such means of amplifying and illustrating a subject would be out of place in scholarly writing, but here a departure from the more formal expository patterns is necessary if the popular article is to hold much appeal for the reader who is motivated less by the desire to be edified, more by the desire to be entertained. And these details are arranged in such a way as to maintain interest at the highest pitch without distorting the subject or misinforming the reader: as unified, swift moving, forcefully stated, climactically ordered explanations and interpretations. The best popular articles are not sophistic, nor are they sensational. The author has simply selected the most provocative details and arranged these in the most tantalizing way consistent with his instructive purpose. For the reader of popular articles is a rapid reader, unwilling to pursue a lengthy and closely reasoned line of thought; he much prefers an article projected largely in terms of a few dramatic illustrations. The following paragraph, like the article on Tahiti from which it is taken, is composed almost entirely of such dramatic illustrations.

> Papeete looks now much as it did in past years, which is to say like a weather-beaten Mexican border town. There are parks with magnificent trees, two-story wooden buildings, a cathedral, and plenty of debris and garbage in the streets. Here and there a new building amid the jumble of Chinese shops calls attention to itself by the gleam of white plaster; the colors of the older buildings are more muted, washed out. It used to be that when you got to Tahiti you went to the Café Vaima on the waterfront, and within an hour you would be included in all the local gossip and everyone you wanted to see would stroll by. Now the pace has picked up beyond a stroll: French military types in short-short pants and loose shirts buzz by on motorcycles, and the girls who would be gossip topics if they were walking careen by so quickly on their Vespas that they do not become a part of what is talked about. The girls are still in bright print *pareus,* golden shoulders bared, the calloused feet either bare or sandaled. When they smile there are not as many gaps as there used to be; more money, more dental work. Gold teeth flash. Exhaust fumes mix with the salt air. There are ocean-going yachts, with their connotations of timelessness and leisure, moored ten yards from the main street. Clothes hang out to dry on the *Iota,* Sydney. Someone is having a cup of instant coffee on the afterdeck of the *Nina,* Honolulu, and someone else is just coming back onto the *Porpoise,* Los Angeles, with some mail. Farther on, at the jetty, the French are creating a naval base; gray LSTs are lined up, disgorging matériel, and

beyond them, American tankers deliver the aviation fuel that keeps the fat Bregeut military cargo planes droning overhead on their way out to the Tuamotus. — George J. W. Goodman, "Tahiti"*

This selection and arrangement of interesting details is complemented in the popular article by *a highly readable, journalistic style.* If you think of style as an indirect expression of the author's personality, his personal idiom, you will find scant evidence of it in the popular article. While you may deduce something of the writer's intellectual turn of mind from the way in which he expresses himself, you can know practically nothing of his private experiences, thoughts, tastes, values. That is to say, the popular article is communication rather than self-expression.

However, the author, in adapting his diction and syntax to the subject and reader, does make stylistic decisions: an article of the Viet Nam war will not use the same language as one written on early eighteenth-century formal gardens; nor will an article on how to roast a wild duck be written in the same way for a woman's magazine as for a man's. But knowing even a great deal about the subject and reader does not provide all the stylistic answers. The author must finally choose his own manner of speaking: an article on poverty may be tough, hard-hitting, angry, or it may be tender, pathetic, sad.

The popular article is of uncertain origin. A form of journalistic prose, its fortunes have been linked with those of the newspaper and magazine. While the article was no doubt a feature of the eighteenth-century periodical, in no century has it been so dominant as in the present. Many regret the tendency for the popular article to replace the essay, sketch, short story, and other more literary forms; but others obviously appreciate the factual and topical article. For better or worse, it has become the dominant prose form of the twentieth century and is largely a product of the twentieth century. The popular article is, indeed, much too widely read and influential a form to be taken lightly. And many competent writers are for one reason or another attracted to the form, even though it carries with it a certain anonymity: the popular article, because it is current, is apt to become dated or irrelevant with the passing of time; the perishable nature of a newspaper or magazine works against the author's lasting reputation; and even though most articles are signed, the author reveals so little of himself that we are, indeed, apt to forget that it was written by a skillful and discriminating personality.

Never wholly the province of hack writers, the popular article is becoming less so as readers become better educated and as more knowledgeable specialists begin seriously to have a go at popular education. Rachael Carson, Bruce Catton, Bernard Devoto, Paul DeKruif, J. Frank Dobie, Fred Gipson, Edith Hamilton, Wolfgang Langewiesche, and Lowell Thomas, to name a few American authors, have all written a great many popular articles. Since the foreign periodical does not often come into our hands, we rarely get to know the English writers of popular articles as well, but you have perhaps read the work of Harold Nicholson, V. S. Pritchett, C. P. Snow, and Fred Hoyle.

And it is a fact that in the nineteenth and twentieth centuries the writer has generally come from a journalistic background. In the era from Mark Twain to Hemingway it is difficult to think of one that didn't: Stephen Crane, Theodore Dreiser, James Thurber, Sinclair Lewis, Sherwood Anderson, H. L. Mencken, E. B. White . . . even playwrights, like Eugene O'Neill, Robert Sherwood, and Maxwell Anderson . . . and poets, like Carl Sandburg, all served their apprenticeship on a newspaper or magazine. So there is much of the popular article in modern literature. And the enthusiasm of the reading audience for popular articles on science, history, biography, travel, national and international affairs, domestic and office problems will continue to attract competent writers — especially those who wish to improve society by educating and informing the public.

How to Write the Popular Article

Because it is written with journalistic fidelity to fact and would communicate detailed truth to a reader in the most compelling way, considerable planning is involved in writing the popular article. Indeed, method is more important than sheer writing ability.

1) Even though you may already have a subject in mind, you must at the outset *form the clearest possible picture of your reader.* Your article will never find its audience unless you find it first — before the article is written. There are two ways of getting to know your reader: First, take whatever opportunities come along to learn the interests, tastes, values, motives, prejudices, hopes, fears of the class of people to which you expect to address yourself — sound people out on these subjects, try putting yourself in the other fellow's place to look at life through his eyes, cultivate the arts of listening and observing. And second, study the ways in which well-edited magazines appeal to what they consider their particular audience. You must become a kind of arm-chair psychologist and social scientist, a student of at least a part of the human race.

2) *Look about for subjects that would likely interest such a class of readers.* Biography, history, travel and places, scientific progress, useful information, how-to-do-it, exposés or other controversial matters are all areas to consider. The best subjects are suggested by personal experience (college classes, hobbies, work) and by reading (many times another popular article which left you with a desire to know more). And the best subjects are often near at hand. The impression that articles are most often written on odd and unusual subjects is a false one. The great majority are on surprisingly familiar and commonplace subjects — revealed, to be sure, in a new light. Wordsworth's practice in poetry of making the plain forms and facts of life appear marvelous is quite as applicable to the popular article. The reader of popular articles is a person of mundane interests. His preoccupations are with this world and this life of his. You must, of course, make a point of telling him

something he does not already know, or he will not consider reading on. But the subject itself must be something he immediately recognizes as timely and relevant to his experience.

3) *Appraise your reader's interest in this particular subject.* There are three important reasons for making such a check: to see if the subject is worth pursuing, to decide what aspect to take up, and to decide how to approach it. For each article assignment, at least until you are somewhat experienced, make a brief written analysis of your prospective reader. Include age, sex, cultural level, previous knowledge, appeals the subject holds for the reader, and any other pertinent information. (If the popular article is to be turned in as an assignment, be sure it is accompanied by this description of the reader — especially if the article is not written for the class of readers represented by the students and the instructor.) Most of your planning will be based on what this reveals about your reader's relation to the subject.

4) Now you are ready to *decide what the specific subject and thesis will be.* Every article has a definite subject, a topic you can explore for this reader in this many pages in a satisfying way. Remember, the popular article relies on facts and illustrations; be sure that your subject is restricted enough that you can concentrate on specific details rather than generalizations. And every article has, for the sake of unity and purpose, a definite thesis, a statement which sums up the central idea of your article in a single sentence. If, for example, you wished to write a popular article on the early days of aviation, you might choose as your subject, "Wiley Post," and as your tentative thesis, "In proving the usefulness of the automatic pilot, radio direction finder, variable pitch propeller, and other systems, Wiley Post became the first of the world's true scientific test pilots." The thesis of a popular article is usually fresh and provocative. It would be pointless for it to be self-evident, though a general truth is sometimes worth expressing if the specific illustrations are sufficiently interesting. There is rarely any reason to be indirect in stating the thesis, unless the article is on an extremely controversial subject, and defends or proposes the unpopular view, or unless good taste forbids too

explicit phrasing of the thesis — but exceptions to a matter-of-fact statement of the thesis are extremely rare. In any case, write out the thesis now, clearly and specifically. See if you can come up with a simple declarative sentence which not only names and limits the subject, but summarizes and concludes the entire article as well.

5) Since the popular article is factual and informative, you will undoubtedly have to *do a certain amount of information gathering.* The subject itself may have been suggested by some personal observation or experience, but unless you are an expert writing about your speciality, you will have to gather more material before going any further in your planning. Begin by taking inventory of what you already know about the subject. From there contrive how to get the information you need. Perhaps the library can supply all you need to know, but the writer of popular articles must often ask questions, interview, simply go and see for himself. Remember this about the popular article: while facts and figures are essential, details which stimulate human interest are equally important. So in gathering information about the subject, look for anecdotes, analogies, illustrations, examples that will lead the reader to appreciate the implications of the facts in familiar human situations and thereby vivify and enliven the article.

6) You may find it useful to *make a quick preliminary or inventory outline.* While this will not be quite the shape the article finally takes, such a brief outline will indicate where you need to fill out your popular article by gathering information. And even at this stage you should begin thinking of the five, six, or seven topics upon which the article will be based. A popular article on shell collecting, for example, could easily be written around these topics:

— Beginning: The simple beauty of seashells — shape and texture, color and pattern. Thesis: The seashell has, because of its simple and evocative beauty and the ease with which it is preserved and displayed, long been valued by collectors of natural objects.

— Common but beautiful shells

— Rare and valuable shells

— The earliest "collectors" (shells as utensils, currency, decoration, and objects of worship)

— The beginning of serious shell collecting in the 17th century

— Ending: the modern collector

7) After the brief outline comes *the full outline*. An outline holds you to a plan, presents the results of your research and other preliminary thinking in the most accessible way, discloses any major weakness in your conception of the article at a stage where it can be most easily corrected. The more extensive the outline the better — a noun-phrase or sentence outline will serve you best.

This outline is, of course, predicated on some knowledge of the popular article as a form. While you will not actually use these terms, it is useful to outline your article in terms of its beginning, middle, and end, with the proportions of something between 1:3:1 and 1:9:1.

8) The *beginning* of a popular article is almost invariably direct, it identifies the subject and in almost every case states the thesis without any delay. Professional writers speak of the beginning of a popular article as having two parts: the "lead" and the "transition." The *lead* is an arresting allusion to the subject and perhaps the thesis, one which at the same time demonstrates their relevance to the reader's experience. It may be a forceful statement, a pointed question, a quick summary, a provocative description or narrative — anything that is reasonably striking and to the point. Some leads, like the following paragraph, are dramatically compelling.

> It strikes without warning, usually before dawn, jolting its victim awake. Throbbing pulses of pain grip his big toe. Instinctively, he flexes his joint, only to feel the stabbing, searing pains shoot up his leg. Now the slightest movements, even the vibrations of a passing car, provoke new surges of anguish. And he knows, if he has suffered through similar attacks, that he is in for days — perhaps weeks — of contin-

uous torture. — Albert Q. Maisel, "An End, at Last, to Gout?"*

Obvious tricks to shock the reader into attention will not win you an audience — but neither will a flat, pedestrian lead. The *transition* does just what the term implies: it leads the reader into the discussion, the body of the article. Often you will need to explain the connection between the lead — which looks ahead to the article's conclusion — and the point at which you begin the article proper. At any rate, in the beginning you want to focus the reader's attention on the subject of your article and suggest what direction it will take.

In the following beginning of a popular article, the subject is clearly "steam locomotives," and the thesis "each railway has designed engines to suit its own particular needs" — the first paragraph and a half comprising the lead, and the last two sentences of the second paragraph forming the transition. (The article will go on to discuss locomotives having a "wholly South African 'style' ".)

To many the steam locomotive is the very essence of railroading. Since the time of the first railroads, some 150 years ago, steam has propelled trains from one corner of the earth to the other. In South Africa the first steam locomotive, weighing just 14 tons, arrived at Cape Town in 1859. A hundred years later the South African Railways were taking delivery of giants weighing over 190 tons.

The steam locomotive has never been a mass-produced machine in the modern sense. Instead, each railway has designed engines to suit its own particular needs. In South Africa the railway gauge is 3′ 6″, narrow by European and North American standards. Coupled with this are geographical conditions involving vast distances through rugged mountains and inhospitable deserts. — Allen A. Jorgensen, "On Puff the Billies, On and On . . ."†

* Excerpt from "An End, at Last, to Gout?," by Albert Q. Maisel. *The Reader's Digest*, June 1967. Used with permission.

† From *South African Panorama*, March, 1967. Reprinted by permission of *South African Panorama* and the author.

9) The *middle* of the popular article is, of course, that comparatively lengthy section in which the main work of the article is done. The materials are selected and arranged according to your purpose and your appraisal of the reader. Although you will not go about it with quite the directness of the newspaper reporter, the who-what-when-where-why-how of your subject now becomes imperative. The popular article is, after all, informative prose. The subject itself may suggest an approach; most by their very nature imply one of the traditional forms of order: spatial, chronological, cause-and-effect, emphatic. But often you have an alternative, and to say anything new on any subject you may need to consider something other than the inevitable. And certainly you will try to arrange your materials in terms of increasing relevance and importance, the earlier topics being for the most part preliminary to the later ones.

But the greatest problem for most writers is striking the right balance between generalizations and particulars. For example, while statistics are more significant than individual cases, most readers find the latter more appealing. The proportion depends on the subject and the reader, but certainly whatever you wish to say in a popular article must be projected largely as illustrations, examples, anecdotes, details which involve the reader in a way abstract generalizations could not. Throughout the middle you will alternate between the two ways of presenting information to keep the article varied and interesting, a statistic or other generalization followed by one or more specific illustrations. Too much generalization will lose your reader; too much specific detail will lose the overall conception of your subject. The more informed and motivated your reader, the better equipped he will be to absorb statistics and other generalizations. But every effective article must be richly provided with specific detail.

Notice in the following two paragraphs from the middle of a popular article how each generalization is clearly illustrated:

> The test to be applied, when a new word is suggested or it is sought to give an old word a new meaning, is this: Does the change enrich the language? The easiest and silliest way in which to impoverish the language is to misuse a

> good existing word that conveys a clear and precise meaning and thereby to destroy that meaning and render the word useless. This is what Americans have done by using "alibi" when they mean "excuse." An alibi can never be an excuse, and an excuse can never be an alibi. A man pleads an alibi when he denies that he did an act and says that he could not have done it, since he was elsewhere (alibi) at the time. By an excuse, on the other hand, he admits the act, but says there was a good reason for it. The distinction should really not be too difficult for the ordinary intelligence to grasp. The misuse is a barbarism which has made the language poorer by depriving it of a once-useful word. It is like spoiling a chisel by using it as a screwdriver. It is linguistic murder.
>
> Let me pass from American murder to American pretentious illiteracy; from the destruction of an old word to the invention of a new word which clearly cannot bear the meaning assigned to it. "Underprivileged" is the leading example. This word appears to be used as a synonym for "poor," a word which strikes many Americans as mildly improper, though I do not know whether they propose to rewrite the Beatitudes. I have found in many conversations that, while they understand the criticism that the word "underprivileged" is pretentious, they do not see immediately that it is illiterate, but it demonstrably is. A privilege is a special advantage which one person has over another or one class over another class. It is an inequality before the law. An underprivileged person must mean a person who has not enough privilege — a person, that is to say, who has not enough advantage over his neighbor. To pretend that you are in favor of equality before the law and then to use a word which complains that there is not enough inequality seems to me to exceed the stupidity limit.
> — Lord Conesford, "You Americans are Murdering the Language."*

And notice in this paragraph the ways in which a financial figure is made more interesting and significant:

* From *The Saturday Evening Post*, July, 1957. Reprinted by permission of Curtis Brown, Ltd., London.

> The total marine budget for the year beginning with July 1, 1967 amounts to only $462,000,000 — a mere 3 per cent of federal research and development expenditure. However, the main thrust of the work to be financed with this small sum is so pointed (in the direction of providing protein food for exploding populations of hungry lands, speeding transportation through selective use of hydrofoils and air cushion vehicles, and renovating cities by sculpting their waterfronts) that the effect is bound to be comparable to the renaissance that accompanied the sailings of the clipper ships in the early nineteenth century. — John Lear, "Exploration Race: Moon or Sea?"*

10) The *ending* either summarizes or concludes the article. If it is a summary ending, it should not be a tedious repetition, but a quick and revealing epitome, fresh because the reader sees for the first time the summation of the whole. If it is a conclusion ending, it will of necessity be something new. Whichever ending you use, summary or conclusion, the nucleus of the ending is the restatement of the thesis. Having said it at least once before, at the beginning, this final statement of the thesis should certainly be more emphatic and sweeping. You may choose to end the article here, or you may go on to show that the thesis illustrates some greater truth about life, or you may vividly remind your reader of the relevance of the thesis by concluding with some illustrative material or an anecdote. Here are two endings — the first is a short summary ending:

> It is certainly true that young people, speaking in a language of their own out of their special isolated world, have concepts different from ours with respect to love, marriage, work, war, racial relations, education, time, money, and whatever it is we mean when we speak of the American Way of Life. But the fact that their concepts are different does not always mean that they are correct, or even that the youngsters who espouse them actually believe in them. Like as not, the young people are trying to test them, and in any case our

* From *Saturday Review*, March 4, 1967. Reprinted by permission of *Saturday Review*.

response cannot simply be to be scandalized and go "arrgh," but rather to try to figure out who these new people are, and how they got that way, and what they are saying that might be valuable; to give them the listening ear they most often badly need, and tell them what we think as plainly and as honestly as we can, whether they will like it or not.

It is not always easy to do this when a language barrier exists and when the concepts seem so different, but the fact that it is difficult to do something does not always mean that it is unnecessary to do it. And that, by the way, is a concept a good many young people seem never to have considered. — John Keats, "Talking Across the Generation Barrier."*

The second is a short conclusion ending:

Our studies thus far indicate that the moose and wolf populations on Isle Royale have struck a reasonably good balance. It seems likely that, for decades to come, the voice of primitive America will still be heard on winter nights on a remote wilderness island in Lake Superior. — Durward L. Allen and L. David Mech, "Wolves Versus Moose on Isle Royale."†

11) Now *look over your beginning, middle, and ending as you have outlined them.* Every idea and example should be accounted for. The transformation of an outline into an article is purely verbal. You will add some minor details, to be sure, but most of the expansion will be a result of your having added the words necessary to making an effective and pleasing prose statement. In short, it should be patently clear from the outline exactly what you will be writing at every point. To do this your outline will probably have to be from one-third to one-half as long as the final article.

As you assess the usefulness of your outline ask yourself

* Reprinted from "Talking Across the Generation Barrier" by John Keats, in the July, 1967 issue of *Family Circle Magazine*. © The Family Circle Inc., 1967. Reprinted also by permission of the author.

† From *National Geographic*, February, 1963. Copyright by the National Geographic Society, Washington, D.C. All rights reserved.

these pertinent questions: First, is it all there? Outlines are naturally sketchy, but many times they are so far short of suggesting how an adequately developed article is to be written that they need to be expanded. You may need to expand your treatment of the subject *horizontally*, by adding on other related ideas, as in the following paragraph:

> However, in Arizona today, and to a lesser extent in Alaska and elsewhere, everybody wants dams, or thinks he wants dams, like a panacea, or religion — to guarantee a better life, thus inducing increased bank deposits, freeway construction, congestion and sprawl. Where there should be fundamental research into problems of water storage and comprehensive long-range planning, political hysterics prevail. Harnessing natural features and improving upon rivers represent man's splendid ingenuity, beyond a doubt. But the greater ingenuity is to show that man can survive while leaving some few features of the earth to their own devices. This is the true test of our mechanical, intellectual and moral skills. — Michael Frome, "The Politics of Conservation."*

Or you may need to expand *vertically*, by going into the idea (analysis, detail, illustration), as in this paragraph:

> The social scientists have helped make the U.S. the most self-analytic civilization ever known. Rome was not conscious of the "fall of the Roman Empire"; the Crusaders scarcely analyzed the infectious new ideas they brought back from the East; the romantics wrote new kinds of poetry, but did not turn out essays on the alarming death wishes in those poems. Americans cannot make a move without having it declared a trend, viewed critically in innumerable books deploring *The Lonely Crowd, The Status Seekers, The Organization Man*. The exhortations offered to the U.S. public are always contradictory. No sooner had Americans learned that they must not be rugged individualists but must practice "adjustment," than they were told that they were all turning into conformists. No sooner had they learned that children must be raised progressively and permissively than they were told that children

* From *Holiday*, February, 1967. Reprinted by permission of the author.

> **desperately want discipline. No sooner had they accepted the fact that women deserved and needed equal rights than they were informed that women had become too much like men. — "The Anatomy of *Angst*."***

Also you may have started or stopped too soon and dealt with too few events or ideas; or you may have skipped over certain events or ideas essential to the sequence. Second, is it in the right order? Whatever scheme of order you choose, be sure that it is reasonable in view of the subject and your purposes, and that you stick to it. The reader should feel a sense of inevitability in the way these thoughts occur in this order. And third, is the relation of topics or parts clear? Later on you will have to worry about the smoothness of your transitions, but transitions can't do everything. At this point make sure that the ideas are such the reader can move easily from one to the next.

12) Since you are working from a rather extensive outline, you will need only *flesh out the discussion and add transitions to have a rough draft.* Follow the outline closely. If it proves inadequate, you had better revise the outline before going any further with your writing. But don't be bound by the tentative and abbreviated style of the outline. Even if you are working from a sentence outline, you should find yourself translating even those sentences into something more elaborate and felicitous.

See to it that every sentence is connected to the sentence that follows and the sentence that precedes, and that every paragraph is connected to the paragraphs that precede and follow, and that every major unit of the design and order of the article is connected with the preceding unit and with the following unit. A connection, or transition, must be of size enough to serve the units being connected. A single word may connect one sentence with another, even one short paragraph with another. But a unit of several paragraphs may need an entire sentence to connect to another unit of several paragraphs. In longer essays, paragraphs themselves may become transitional and connective.

13) Undoubtedly you have given some thought to a *title* before now, but this is a good time to do so seriously. The best titles for popular articles are short (ideally two or three words), descriptive, and provocative. But since the most descriptive titles are rarely short, you will probably find yourself compromising. Try one and then another, listening to the sound of it each time, until you come up with something that would be consistent with the article's purpose and at the same time would stimulate a browsing reader to pick it up.

14) Although you have kept the reader in mind all along, *take a critical look at the article you have written and the audience that will read it* — asking yourself, is it everywhere absolutely clear and compelling reading? Vagueness and dullness are death to the popular article. And these are not conditions you can recognize in your own work unless you can put yourself in the reader's place. Of all readers, yours are the most critical because they relate the article to their own experience and to the world's realities, expecting to discover something that is useful and true.

An Exemplary Popular Article

Help Wanted: 50,000 Programmers

GENE BYLINSKY

Many companies that have invested in the latest-model computers find themselves increasingly frustrated by the discrepancy between the fantastic potential of the machines and their own ability to use them with maximum effectiveness. Within a short twenty years computer electronics has gone through a phenomenal revolution: vacuum tubes have given way to transistors, which in turn are being displaced by micro-miniaturized solid-logic circuitry, dramatically boosting computation speeds and the size of computer memories. But these leaps in technology have outdistanced the techniques of organizing and directing the work of the lightning-fast machines. One consequence is an acute shortage of the people who prepare the instructions, or programs, without which the electronic "brains" won't run or do useful work.

Computer programmers have been in short supply "from Day One," as one man puts it. But today the shortage is worse than ever. About 100,000 men and women are employed as programmers in the U.S., and there are openings for at least 50,000 more. Column after column of newspaper advertisements exhort high-school graduates and housewives to take up the calling, or tempt specialists already in the field to move on to better jobs. Corporations and independent operators have opened special schools to teach the arcane skills of the profession, and they do not hesitate to raid one another's student bodies. "Everybody is trying to pirate programmers from you all the time," says a Du Pont executive.

The competition has driven salaries up so fast that programing has become probably the country's highest-paying technological occupation. A man (or woman) with two years' experience in programing can make $8,000 to $10,000 a year; four years' experience, even without a college degree, can pay off at $15,000 a year, while advanced specialists can sign on for $20,000 and more. Recruiters for employment agencies active in the field have been known to get bonuses of $2,000 and more for locating a particularly skilled specialist. Even so, some companies can't find experienced programmers at any price.

Programmers are in demand because they produce the "software," the stuff that turns an electronic computer from an inert complex of metal into a versatile tool capable of performing an endless variety of jobs. Software encompasses not only "application" programs, which present a business or scientific problem in a form a computer can understand, but also the great variety of detailed and voluminous instructions stored in computer memory to organize and automate the work of the machine — instructions that make it possible for a computer to be a problem-solving machine in the first place. The tools of software are the various computer languages, or codes, as well as the programs that translate these codes into more basic machine instructions. In short, the programmer deals, in one way or another, with all the functions and techniques of computer operation that depend directly and intimately on human participation.

What, precisely, a programmer does has always been something of a mystery to most people. The jargon of the trade, with its loose use of ill-defined terms, has been in part responsible for the confusion. But there is something elusive about the very nature of programing. "Hardware" is there for all to see. Its construction is a relatively straightforward process. But generating software is "brain business," often an agonizingly difficult intellectual effort. It is not yet a science, but an art that lacks standards, definitions, agreement on theories and approaches. Its component parts can be maddeningly imprecise. "There are ninety ways to write a program," says one practitioner.

At the same time, programing, or software production, has emerged as the most expensive, most problem-plagued component of the $6-billion-a-year electronic data-processing business. Big computer users such as the federal government now spend more on programmers' salaries and on programs than they spend on leasing or buying the computers themselves. And while problems do crop up in hardware from time to time, it is generally agreed that 90 per cent of the troubles that come up in computers today are in programing.

A computer's "hotel staff"

Industry's hunger for capable programmers has been aggravated not only by the rapid proliferation of computers — about 35,000 of all sizes are in use today — but also by their increasing sophistication. On today's fastest models, a problem that used to occupy a machine for an hour can now be run off in three or four seconds. But whereas the "primitive" computers of the early 1950's could be plugged in and almost immediately applied to a specific task, an immense amount of work goes into the big present-day models before they can begin to function. Their inner workings are coordinated by "control" programs of incredible complexity — programs that in some cases contain millions of instructions. These are stored in the computer's memory, and on magnetic tape or disks, as part of what is called the operating system. This system can be likened to a skillful hotel staff. It regulates the flow of jobs inside the computer, assigns storage space for data, delivers messages from one memory location to another, and controls the work of input-output devices such as printers or graphic displays. It also provides a translating service — in the form of "compilers," special programs inscribed on punched cards, magnetic tape, or disks. A compiler acts somewhat like an interpreter at the United Nations; it translates simplified programing codes into the numerical machine language needed to produce the desired action.

Organizing a Beethoven symphony

The men who design and write the operating systems, compilers, and other basic software are the high priests of programing. They are known as systems programmers and are employed mainly by the computer manufacturers and by the so-called "software houses," independent enterprises that have sprung up by the dozen to help fill the need for systems and application software. It's not unusual for a big computer manufacturer to employ hundreds of programmers to design a new operating system.

This massive attack on systems software poses difficult management problems. On the one hand, a good programmer, like a writer or a composer, works best independently. But the pressures to turn out operating systems and other programs within a limited time make it necessary to deploy huge task forces whose coordination becomes a monstrous task. The problem is further complicated by the fact that there is no single "best way" to write either a systems or an application program, or any part of such program. Programing has nowhere near the discipline of physics, for example, so intuition plays a large part. Yet individual programmers differ in their creative and intuitive abilities. Carl Reynolds, president of Computer Usage Development Corp., a subsidiary of Computer Usage Co., Inc., a firm specializing in software, illustrates the problem by asking. "How successful would Beethoven have been if he had had five people work on five parts of a symphony, after giving them some rules of harmony and notation?"

Obviously, the different parts of an operating system should be produced at the same time, and when a customer buys a computer it should come equipped with the control programs needed to make it run. But in their rush to send new computer models to market, the manufacturers haven't been able to keep up with the production and delivery of the support software. Frequently, a customer buys a computer but doesn't get the compiler, or some other important part of the operating system, until six months or a year later. In some cases highly skilled computer users, such as university groups, have gone ahead and written their own portions of operating systems. But most business users of computers, less skilled in the technology of software, have been left to the manufacturers' mercy. As a result they have been forced to tie up their skilled personnel in getting the new machines to operate with the partial, and sometimes faulty, control programs.

Before a computer is put to use on a specific job, such as processing a payroll or calculating the orbit of a satellite, the application programmers go into action. With more and more computers in operation — and being assigned an increasing variety of jobs — application programing has been a rapidly proliferating field. It is here that most corporations feel the pinch of the programmer shortage. Their manpower problem is aggravated by the fact that when they buy newer computers, they have to rewrite their existing application programs to suit the configurations and the logic of the new machines — a time-consuming job that demands battalions of programmers.

The manufacturers have tried to bridge the support software gap with a device called an "emulator," a piece of auxiliary hardware that imitates the logic of an older computer on a new one. It allows the owner of the newest computer to process his data faster than he could on the older machine, but not as fast as he could if the new model were directed by programs that could exploit its full potential. It's a little like equipping a transonic airplane with propeller engines. The emulator obviously is a stop-gap device, but because of the shortage of programmers, some computer users expect to keep on employing it for years to come.

An $18-million hyphen

The programmer begins by analyzing his problem, laying out the logical steps to a solution, and transcribing them onto flow charts. He thus constructs a sort of problem-solving road map for the computer. "Programing is like writing music," says one specialist.

"There are very limited figures with which you can deal. You have to express the problem in sequences and combinations of these figures." Total precision in writing a program is vital, he adds, since the computer blindly executes the instructions given it. "You can't settle for 99.9 per cent accuracy. You're either absolutely all right or all wrong."

Because of the vast number of detailed instructions involved, mistakes are hard to avoid. The more obvious errors can be detected during "debugging" or trial runs by a special "diagnostic" program in the computer's control system; this takes apart the grammar and syntax of the instruction language. The computer may be programed to respond to a simple error by printing out the words "Illegal procedure," or "Parenthesis left off," and sometimes a more irreverent "You dope, you missed a comma."

But there is no way as yet to program a computer to detect semantic errors that can dramatically alter the intent of the program. The amount of damage that even a seemingly minute programing error can do was dramatically demonstrated over Cape Kennedy a few years ago. An Atlas-Agena rocket blasted off the launch pad, carrying what was intended to be the first U.S. spacecraft to fly by Venus. The rocket got about ninety miles above earth when it started wandering erratically and had to be blown up by command from the control center below. Later analysis showed that a mathematician had inadvertently left out a hyphen in writing the flight plan for the spacecraft; in this case the hyphen was a symbol standing for a whole formula. It must have been history's costliest hyphen, for an $18,500,000 rocket was lost.

Another factor that influences the quality of programing is the frequent inability of business and industrial managers to state fully or precisely the problem they want their programmers to solve. "There's a tremendous gap between what the programmers do and what the managers want, and they can't express these things to each other," says Reynolds of Computer Usage. "You know how difficult it is for people in the same field to understand each other perfectly. Here you have one man dealing with symbols and another who is not interested in symbols but wants results."

Partly because of this communication failure and partly because of deadline pressures, all significant programing problems turn out to be emergencies. In many companies, programmers faced with a deadline have been known to spend nights in their offices, catching a few hours' sleep on couches. "They think, 'Just one more hour and I can fix it,' " says Reynolds. "But they can't, and then it's 'one *more* hour.' "

The translation of a problem into a specific form that can be understood by a computer is a process somewhat akin to puzzle solving, but far more challenging and intriguing, for there is no prescribed solution. The best programmers strive for brevity, trying to produce a program that contains the smallest possible number of instructions and will make a computer operate most effectively. Since programing skill varies, there are great variations in efficiency. "A job can be done in one-tenth of the time with a superior program," says Paul Herwitz, director of programing resources at I.B.M.

You don't have to be a mathematician

It doesn't take much special talent to master a simplified programing code, and the ability to consider a problem in logical sequence is not confined to mathematicians. This would seem to indicate that almost anyone who can think logically, has an immense interest in detail, in seeing things through to completion, and has some imagination, can become a programmer. "There isn't an ideal programmer any more than there is an ideal writer," says Reynolds. "All sorts of people, from divinity to mathematics students to music and romance-language majors have gravitated to programing."

Basic programing is so easy to learn that some high schools include it in their curricula. Specialists predict that in a few decades the skill will be as widespread as the ability to drive a car. But although there are a few systems analysts and programing executives without college degrees, it's generally agreed that a person with a scientific or technical training has a better chance to advance to the top of the field than a high-school graduate who has simply been taught elementary coding.

To rise to the ranks of the systems analysts, the elite of the profession, a man not only has to master the technique of translating detailed instructions into a machine code, he must also be able to grasp concepts and to define the over-all, organized, systematic approach to the solution of a problem, or series of problems. And if he's to work with scientific or technical problems, he has to have the background to cope with the subject matter.

Men with such qualifications aren't easy to come by. The best recruits are recent graduates of colleges that offer courses in programing. More than sixty universities now offer such courses. But there are serious deficiencies in the way the subject is taught, since capable instructors are hard to find and textbooks rapidly become outdated. This is why some companies have found it necessary to start their own programing schools, or to send their trainees to the schools that computer manufacturers, such as I.B.M. and R.C.A., operate for their customers.

Once a man is taught the skills, he may be hard to keep. Companies that use their computers for unromantic commercial purposes risk losing their programmers to more glamorous fields such as space exploration. There is "a drift toward the exotic" among programmers, as Elmer C. Kubie, president of Computer Usage Co., puts it. As he explains it, "Computer professionals seem to take substantial pride in their work being 'far out' rather than taking pride in quality craftsmanship of high utilitarian value. It's possible that the fellow working on an inventory-control or commission-analysis program for a used-car dealer has a problem as complex logically, or perhaps even more complex, than the programmer associated with the lunar project. Unfortunately, however, his wife or girl friend won't understand this and, in fact, very few people will. So somehow, the fellow working on the moon project is a near genius, while his counterpart working for the used-car dealer is pretty ordinary."

In general, too, the gifted specialists prefer to work on systems software rather than application programs, because preparation of a control program usually demands greater technical skill and offers a bigger intellectual challenge. In organizing the basic circuitry and memory of computers, the systems programmer works with symbols that approximate the binary code of zeros and ones. A tiny ferrite core in a computer memory is either "on" or "off"; it is switched "on" by a "one" signal and "off" by a "zero." In a modern computer, the systems programmer has to manipulate millions of these memory cores — and at the same time see to it that his portion of the work is integrated into the whole system.

At first, just a supercalculator

The application programmer, on the other hand, isn't principally concerned with directing computer circuits and memories, but with solving problems. At his disposal are "high-level" programing languages that enable him to write a program without knowing how the machine works. The emergence of these "high-level" programing languages made it possible for people without a background in mathematics or computer logic to become application programmers. Indeed, the development of these languages is one aspect of software in which progress has been as remarkable as the revolution in hardware.

In the beginning, programing was to a great extent literally physical work. In designing new machines, man seldom makes a complete break with the past. Just as the first automobile was patterned after the horse-drawn carriage, the first electronic computers imitated mechanical calculators. They were simply calculators that were designed to operate, in effect, on the same program for a long time.

Moreover, the circuits of these primitive computers were very limited in number and scope. The circuits of the first electronic data-processing machine, ENIAC (Electronic Numerical Integrator and Computer), had to be physically rewired for each new problem. Scientists laboriously replugged wire terminals to set up the proper loops to execute the desired instructions as electronic pulses. These instructions, in turn, were triggered by tediously prepared programs, spelled out in numerical machine code on punched cards. This involved writing tens of thousands of code numerals. It was as if a housewife had to rewire a washing machine for each load of laundry, and write out numerical instructions besides. "It was a black art," I.B.M.'s Herman Goldstine, a computer pioneer who worked on the ENIAC, recalled recently. "The chances for mistakes were prodigious."

Seeking a better way to direct the computer's work, Goldstine, in collaboration with the great mathematician, the late John von Neumann, perfected the concept of the "stored program" — putting the instruction program into the computer's memory. The idea had first been proposed by von Neumann, and separately by John

Mauchly and J. Presper Eckert Jr., the two inventors of the ENIAC. But Mauchly and Eckert couldn't apply it to that machine because it had only a minuscule memory.

Their next computer design did contain a larger memory system. Into it was read an instruction program written by Goldstine and von Neumann, and the concept became a proved success. It radically transformed the nature of computers, greatly improving their efficiency and versatility. The use of stored, alterable instructions to direct the action of the machine is what sets the computer apart from any other mechanism man has ever fashioned.

The early programmers were the scientists and mathematicians who were also the first computer users. Irked by the tedious task of spelling out instructions as endless strings of zeros and ones, they started substituting symbols and abbreviations for the binary numbers. These were called "mnemonics," because they were memory-aiding symbolic abbreviations; for example, the programmer used the symbol "LA" instead of spelling out "01000001," the number that had designated the "load address," a sector of the computer memory.

Lowering the communication barrier

After mnemonics came "macro-instructions." Where mnemonic symbols resulted in one-for-one translation, with each symbol generating one machine command, a macro-instruction was designed to set off a whole series of machine actions. From that base a great stride was taken by an I.B.M. team led by John Backus. In three years of back-breaking labor, which included the writing of 25,000 lines of machine instruction, the group produced the first full-fledged high-level computer language — FORTRAN (Formula Translation).

Designed for scientific and technical problem solving, it lowered the communication barrier between the user and the machine and enlarged the scope of computer applications. Each symbol written in FORTRAN generated as many as twenty instructions to the computer. The new language was a major advance not only because it simplified programing, but also because it launched the efficient use of compilers, or translation programs. The compiler accepted FORTRAN formulas and expressions such as "IF," "DO," and "GO

TO" and translated them into the numerical code that activated the machine. This obviously saved a lot of work for application programmers.

In the first version of FORTRAN the programmer still had to spell out specific instructions for each action of the computer; the command "GO TO 0500," for instance, told the computer to refer to memory location number 0500. But eventually the language underwent a number of revisions that made it more "problem-oriented" rather than "machine-oriented," and other languages have emerged that allow the programmer to concentrate on his problem instead of on instructing the machine. With COBOL (Common Business Oriented Language), for instance, a programmer can write simply "add dividends to income," and the compiler does the rest.

The successful incorporation of some English words and phrases into programing languages inspired the vision of new programing codes so simple that almost anybody could be his own programmer. Predictions of businessmen blithely conversing with their omnipotent machines in plain English still get played up regularly in the press. In fact, however, such notions are grossly overoptimistic. In the opinion of most knowledgeable computer experts, there are severe limits to the use of everyday English to direct computers. English, or any spoken language for that matter, is full of subjective connotations, which an instrument as objective as a computer could not possibly grasp. So the vocabulary would have to be narrowly restricted, and the grammar artificial. The result would be a language with the outward appearance of English but not really comprehensible to the average person. Programmers would still be needed.

Far more efficient tools for instructing the computers are the so-called "shoptalk" languages that are gaining increasing acceptance in specialized fields such as engineering. These make it possible for an engineer to express a problem in the language of his specialty — in formulas, abbreviations, and some English words — bypassing the need for an application programmer. Shoptalk codes may also be developed for some specific business applications, such as inventory control. Another shortcut is the use of graphics, or pictorial input and output, in which one picture presented on a cathode-ray tube can often tell a computer user more than half a ton of numerical printout. This might alleviate the shortage of programmers in fields such as designing of cars or airplanes.

Make the machine do more "thinking"

For the average business user of computers, however, the most promising path to alleviating programing problems is to incorporate many of the software functions into the machine logic itself. Years ago, in fact, computer designers built "logic" circuits into the machines to perform such elementary functions as multiplication, division, and subtraction, which the first computers had been incapable of performing without a programmer's help. (When a user wanted to divide some numbers, for instance, he had to program a division algorithm, or step-by-step rule, for this purpose and feed it into the computer.) The built-in "logic" greatly enlarged the faculties of the electronic "brains," both in speed and in ease of use. More recently, however, this mode of progress was pretty much abandoned, and systems men concentrated their ingenuity on devising even more elaborate programs to accomplish various tasks. Now computer manufacturers in their long-range planning are once again taking a serious look at the concept of making a computer a tool as automatic as, say, a self-service elevator.

Millions of components in a cubic foot

This objective has been made more realistic by the electronic riches of solid-state technology. Hundreds of millions of microminiaturized components could be packed into a cubic foot of computer space, an almost incredible advance over transistor technology, which allowed about 100,000 components per cubic foot. Ponderous control programs could be replaced in new computers by tiny systems that would automatically sort or process data; computer users would finally have in hand a much more resourceful and dependable machine — a machine that ideally could be immediately applied to a specific task.

Whatever happens, it is unlikely that the need for programmers will abate. Indeed, the shortage will probably become more acute, even though by the 1970's training in programing skills will be much more widespread than it is today. The next generation of computers will require more complex operating systems. The number of computers in use in the U.S. is expected to leap from the present 35,000 to 60,000 by 1970 and to 85,000 by 1975. And the range and scope of computer applications will vastly expand. "There is also the possibility that increased complexity of machines will more than counterbalance the improvements in programing efficiency," says one specialist. "The software man will be in even greater demand in 1970 than he is today."

An Analysis

1) To what general class of readers is the article directed?
2) In what magazines other than *Fortune* might this article have appeared?
3) What is the subject of "Help Wanted: 50,000 Programmers"?
4) Does Gene Bylinsky ever state his thesis explicitly in the article proper? Where do you find such one sentence expressions of the article's main point?
5) Does Gene Bylinsky state the thesis more than once? How does the restatement of the thesis in the end differ from that in the beginning?
6) How descriptive is the title, "Help Wanted: 50,000 Programmers"?
7) What is the tone of "Help Wanted: 50,000 Programmers"? Why is tone an important consideration even in such an unemotional article as this?
8) Could you have written this article? How would you have prepared yourself for writing such an article or something like it?
9) How would you describe the general form of the article?
10) Is there a clear lead, transition, middle, and end?
11) What transitions and connections does Gene Bylinsky regularly employ in "Help Wanted: 50,000 Programmers"?
12) Does the author use quotations, examples, images, analogies, metaphors, similes, anecdotes to clarify and vivify his ideas?
13) In what ways is Gene Bylinsky's style journalistic, even though it is rather more formal and deliberate than the style of many popular articles?

Assignments

1) Go to the periodical department of your library, and look at several issues of the same magazine published during the last twenty years, e.g. the January, odd-year issues of *Saturday Evening Post* between 1947 and 1967. What percentage of the fare is made up of popular articles and what percentage is fiction? Has the proportion changed during that time?
2) From a study of the advertising in a particular magazine, what kind of reading audience do you think the magazine is intended to appeal?
3) Write the same basic article for two distinctly different reading audiences.
4) Study a popular article you especially admire. Make a list of how and where you think the writer got each piece of information, "personal experience," "interview," "library research," etc.
5) See if you can turn an encyclopedia article or textbook discussion into an interesting popular article. What examples or illustrations would you probably have to bring from elsewhere in order to make the article compelling reading?
6) Make a structural analysis of a short published popular article, identifying the lead, the transition, the middle, the ending with marginal brackets; circling each clear statement of the thesis; marking statements of general fact with double underlinings and specific details (examples, illustrations, anecdotes, etc.) with a single underlining.
7) List some articles you were led to read principally because of their titles. What about those titles attracted you? Find articles with titles that you think are misleading in one way or another. (The common fault is overstatement, implying that the article and subject are more earth-shaking than they could possibly be.)
8) Read only the first paragraphs of several popular articles. Which of the articles do you really want to finish? What about those leads attracted you? (Of course, most often you choose to read or not read an article because of its

subject; but in a surprising number of instances the real deciding factor was not the subject but how it was introduced.)

9) Find two popular articles on the same subject, one decidedly inferior to the other. List all the reasons why you find the second article inferior. Or if you prefer, list all the reasons why you find the first article superior.

10) Now, in view of what you have learned about the popular article, write such a prose form following as nearly as possible the described procedure.

3

The Professional Article

The professional article is difficult to generalize about since it comprises a number of specialized prose forms — scholarly papers, theses, textbooks, business and technical reports — each involving a special procedure. For the sake of simplicity, we shall limit the discussion to the kind of writing students and teachers are most familiar within an academic framework, the scholarly article — but much of the discussion will apply to any writing of this kind you may do in your scholastic or professional careers.

The Professional Article as a Form

Any reasonably complete description of the professional article must acknowledge that it involves: the critical investigation of a problem or proposition, a closely reasoned and methodically developed structure, and an accurate and learned style.

Since the *critical investigation of a problem or proposition* is the main object of the professional article, it is not surprising that writing one requires rather more preparation than do many prose forms. Indeed, far more of the writer's effort is spent educating himself generally about the subject and researching a particular aspect of it than writing up the results.

The professional article deals with a subject about which the author has some special knowledge or insight, a subject that is often difficult or obscure. And the subject appeals to a reader of somewhat specialized tastes, who for personal and professional reasons wants to be better educated. Thus, the author does not have to show that his subject is relevant, but can get quickly to the heart of the matter and concentrate on making a complete and detailed comment on some specific subject about which the reader already has an interest. Moreover, the author's attitude is one of philosophical inquiry. In an utterly disinterested way he wants to get to the bottom of something — answer a question that has puzzled him, explore the implications of some suggestive detail, scrutinize what other men pass over lightly not pausing to question. With luck and effort such an objective and penetrating look at a single, limited topic will lead to the expression of a thought which if not wholly new, is revealed in a new light. The professional article is informative, but sometimes cautiously persuasive; the writer, having proved something to his own satisfaction, would now prove it to the reader as well. All speculative and theoretical scholarship depends on the professional article. For the professional article not only communicates knowledge and reports research, but preserves it as well, not only makes a reasonably independent comment, but along with a great many articles on other facets of the same subject makes a comprehensive statement.

In a prose form intended to enable a writer to make some original comment on a specialized subject for a knowledgeable reader, *a closely reasoned and methodically developed structure is essential.* The reader of a professional article does not have to be courted with quite the same enthusiasm as readers of most other prose forms in order to be won. Accustomed to much sophisticated reading, he is receptive to the article as soon as he recognizes its bearing on a subject of professional interest. Even for this reader the writer must explain and support every statement that is not self-evident, but he need not always feel compelled to be lively and colorful. To exploit the full repertoire of appeals available to the writer takes words and, for this reader, detracts from the main business. Indeed, the reader of professional articles, more concerned with truth than appearances, is likely to become suspicious of what he will regard as condescension or sophistry or lack of objectivity. Consequently, the writer of a professional article is more concerned with presenting convincing evidence rather than simply the most dramatic illustrations. His first responsibility is to his subject, the selection and arrangement of details is made on the basis of pertinence rather than interest — though, happily, for readers of professional articles the two generally coincide. Hence, such serious and concentrated studies of what has heretofore been overlooked or misunderstood are developed as a studious reader expects them to be: deliberate and explicit from the first statement of the subject, problem, and thesis; through the step-by-step presentation of the argument; to the final commentary on the results.

There are, of course, the conventions of scholarship — those accepted forms for presenting footnotes and bibliography, and for preparing the manuscript generally — which have to do with the surface structure of the professional article. A convenience for both writer and reader, and pretty well established over the years, these conventions are a necessary part of scholarly, technical, and professional writing.

It follows that such a formal structure should be matched by an *accurate and learned style*. The style of the professional article is still "plain," though it does employ a professional vocabulary and educated idiom. There is nothing particularly formidable or difficult about it; certainly everything is done to avoid vagueness and obscurity. The author subordinates himself and his stylistic individuality in order to shun subjectivity and emotional connotation. Although scholarly and professional writing is more casual than it once was, and the first person is occasionally used, the third person is still the prevailing viewpoint. The rare instances of pedantry are more a matter of style than of conception; subjects are not in themselves inconsequential or soporific — yet some inept writers are like alchemists in reverse with their knack for turning gold into lead. Professional articles are, indeed, serious and studied, but almost never dull and artificial. The style of the professional article is nothing more than the natural manner of expression for an educated man writing for an educated reader of like interests.

The professional article as we know it could hardly be said to have existed before the establishment of learned and professional journals in the nineteenth century. There are, however, numerous classical examples of scholarly writing which have some of the qualities of the modern prose form. True, they tended to be more sweepingly comprehensive and were often unabashedly theoretical (in this respect more nearly approximating the formal essay); they were less accurate and reasoned; and they were without the paraphernalia associated with modern scholarship — but they fulfilled the same function for the ancients. Later, many of the works of the Scholastics and Encyclopediasts were in essence professional articles. With the establishment of universities in the Middle Ages and founding of royal societies and national academies in the Renaissance, the professional article became more common. And finally, with the extension and complexity of education, the arts and sciences, business and industry in modern times, the professional article became a definite prose form.

In the academic, scientific, and technological world the professional article is the standard form of serious communication. And what many do not realize, the professional article is also a means of preserving knowledge. Research published in the form of a professional article will be accessible indefinitely for interested readers; it achieves a permanence few other short prose forms possess. The journals, reviews, quarterlies, proceedings, monographs, papers published by universities and professional societies are absolutely essential to human intellectual affairs — and the basic form of expression in all these publications is the professional article.

Because professional articles are written not only for today but also for tomorrow, and because they need not adapt to the capricious tastes of the popular reading audience, every effort has been made to find the best possible form for presenting truth as conceived by an original thinker and then to make it by mutual consent the standard of scholarly and scientific communication. The conventions of scholarship are one of the results. Thus, the history of the professional article is unique in that there has been little evolution of the form in the last fifty years and it is not likely to change appreciably in the future.

How to Write the Professional Article

The professional article is a more definite form than many, partly because it is so objective and partly because there are conventions regarding its contents and appearance. If you are not challenged by the prospect of doing any original thinking, and if you are not willing to work up to professional standards, you will find writing the professional article an altogether wearisome experience. You may, indeed, think you have already found it so despite your best intentions. But what you have written were, in fact, trumped-up research papers — cut and paste jobs made up of paraphrases and quotations from the usual obvious sources. The professional article is something else again — and most writers seem to follow this sort of plan.

1) *Begin by reading widely and in depth in some area.* Make it your own; become an authority. This really isn't so impossible as it may seem. (You may know comparatively little about, say, John Donne's poetry; but you could make it a point to know far more than most about the herbs alluded to in his verses, in this way providing another insight into the man's poetic vision.) It would be pointless to write a professional article unless you possessed a thought which seemed to you true and revealing and original. And obviously such thoughts do not come to one who has only superficial knowledge of his subject. The more pressed for time you are, the more directed your reading will have to be. This means you must specialize from the beginning, limit your reading to that which pertains most specifically to your particular interest. Surely your own instincts will lead you to consider the most worthwhile aspects of a subject. Naturally, the obvious and the trivial, the conjectural and the synoptic are not. And if the subject is current,

you will have to depend largely on your own resources for facts and the opinions of others will be scarce. So first learn the basic facts about your subject, and then concentrate on some part about which you might reasonably become a qualified expert.

2) As you read, *cast about for a specific topic,* a facet of the larger subject you find especially provocative and promising. Life is so rich and mysterious and every subject so filled with possibilities that we perpetually try too much, spread ourselves too thin. But to write intelligently for a reader who is already well-informed on the subject, you will have to specialize. In fact, the less you know about the subject to begin with, the more you will have to limit yourself. Providing you know the basic facts about your subject, an intensive knowledge can make up for the lack of an extensive knowledge. Later, after you have come to know your subject better, you will be able to make more comprehensive assertions about it — this may come as a surprise to some students, who, accustomed to thinking the other way round, try to generalize about what they know very little. At any rate, the first object is to concentrate on a topic sufficiently specific that you can become acquainted with a significant part of what has been written about it.

3) And the next object, once you have got the boundaries of what is to be your province clearly marked, is to *begin looking for some hitherto unapparent or unappreciated truth about your subject.* You will probably not discover any such revelation right off, but ultimately you will come across something that will make you pause — a curious fact, an inner contradiction, a suggestive detail, a possible connection. If you are truly interested in the subject (and it would be inconceivable to make such a close study of something that didn't interest you) a great many questions will occur to you in connection with your study. Follow them up. And give yourself time, time for all the reading and thinking that will have to be done before all the pieces begin to fall into place.

4) *Jot down a tentative thesis and a preliminary outline* as soon as you can. At this stage the thesis is little more than a guess, or hunch beginning "I wonder if . . . ?"; and the outline

is more a plan for further reading than the design for a scholarly article. But even here, a thesis should begin to take on the characteristics of one — that is, it should not be a purely personal notion ("John Donne is too obscure for modern readers."), or an impossibly broad thesis ("John Donne's poetic imagery is drawn from virtually every province of English seventeenth-century intellectual life."), or an obvious and indisputable fact ("John Donne was a Metaphysical Poet."), but rather some significant truth that could in the several thousand words you have allowed yourself be explored and defended to the complete satisfaction of your reader.

And even the preliminary outline suggests what direction you presume your argument will take and what evidence you expect to present in defense of your proposition. Be prepared for surprises. You may not find what you expect at all. In which case you will either make whatever changes necessary in your thesis, abandon it for a more promising one you discover along the way, or give it up altogether as a false or unsupportable conclusion. Armed with a thesis and outline — though both will be considerably revised later on — you can begin doing concentrated work.

5) *Now read further and compile a bibliography.* Some would begin taking notes at this point, and they would be premature on two counts. For one thing, there is much to be said for reading and thinking about your subject, in light now of your tentative thesis, a while longer before committing yourself. Try as we might to stay flexible, our thoughts on any subject tend to stiffen once we decide what our line is going to be. Even eminent scholars are guilty of hastiness here. So mull over your subject for a spell.

You will do a more discriminating job of research and come up with sounder evidence to support your thesis if you consider the problem of bibliography at the outset. Books, articles, and other items which comprise your bibliography are not by any means your only source of evidence, but they are relied upon so extensively by writers of professional articles that the term "source" has come to imply written works. There is an important distinction to be made between "primary" and "secondary" sources. A *primary source* is the most immediate written revelation of the subject. For the biographer this would include letters and diaries, for the historian eye-witness accounts and contemporary records, for the literary critic the work itself — in short, the subject itself or the most direct expression of the subject. A *secondary source* is the subject as reviewed and commented upon in writing by others. And for the biographer this would include impressions of the person by those who knew him and other biographies, for the historian contemporary views and subsequent histories, for the literary critic reviews and criticism — all interpretations which incorporate a good deal of opinion if not bias. (Of course, if your subject were the changing image of George Washington as reflected in major biographies of several decades, then the various biographies would be primary sources. What is secondary in one instance can be primary in another. And the same is true of the parts of any written work. A direct quotation in a biography would be considered primary even though the biography in general would be secondary.)

You will have the greatest opportunity for original thinking and the least chance of perpetuating the errors of others if you make it your practice to rely as much as possible on primary sources. And when you do depend on secondary sources, be certain that you cite opinions which are either prevailing or authoritative. (The best secondary sources are generally the recently published and highly specialized.)

What you want at this stage is a list of books and articles on your subject drawn from the card catalogue, the periodical indexes, the published bibliographies, the source footnotes and bibliographies in the written works you consult. Look these over, deciding what is most pertinent and significant. (The more discriminating you are here, the less time you will waste when you begin taking notes. And for each source you expect to use, jot down the author, title, and facts of publication on a separate 3″x 5″ card.

— For a book: the author's name reversed, followed by a period; the title of the book, underlined and followed by a period (italicized in print); the place of publication, followed by a colon, then the name of the publisher, followed by a comma; the date of publication, followed by a period.

```
Ardrey, Robert.
The Territorial Imperative.
New York:  Atheneum,
1966.
```

—For an article (essay, story, poem): the author's name reversed, followed by a period; the title of the article, enclosed in quotation marks and followed by a comma (before the closing quotation marks!); the title of the work in which the article appears, underlined and followed by a comma, then the volume number; the date of publication, in parentheses, followed by a comma; and finally the pages on which the article appears, followed by a period.

```
Koenig, Marie.
"Celtic Coins:  A New Interpretation,"
Archaeology, XIX
(January, 1966),
24-30.
```

(There are, needless to say, many published sources that will require a slightly different description. To handle these variations, you may need to consult one of the many guides to scholarly writing.) On the lower half of the card you may wish to jot down a brief description of what you find most useful in this particular source. At any rate, having compiled a tentative bibliography, you will find it much easier to read, take notes, prepare the source footnotes and final bibliography.

6) *Now revise your tentative thesis and preliminary outline in light of what you now know about the subject.* Does your

basic proposition still appear true and worth expressing? Has your reading exposed it as platitudinous or unsupportable? Is your basic line of thought clear and complete? Has your reading disclosed any omissions or any confusion in the present order of your argument? After making whatever revisions are necessary, you are ready to begin work in earnest on the professional article.

7) *Take notes;* there is no alternative. Those who don't wind up starting from scratch, as if they were the first ever to give the subject any thought, the first to write a word about it; or else condemn themselves to endless thumbing through a canyon of books looking for first one and then another vaguely remembered but absolutely essential fact. And there is no more convenient way to record the facts and ideas that will later be incorporated into your article than by jotting each down on a 3″ x 5″ (or 4″ x 6″) card. The utility of such a system is that later you can select and arrange the cards to jibe with your final working outline and write the article with all your materials at hand. To be useful, each card must contain three items: a brief bibliographical tag in the upper left hand corner (since you have a separate bibliographical file the briefest identification is all that is necessary—the author's last name and a page number is usually sufficient), a tentative heading in the upper right hand corner (tentative because it is either a heading from the preliminary outline or simply suggested by the contents of the note), and the note itself consisting, and this is important to remember, of a single fact or idea.

```
Empson, p. 12
          The pastoral as a form of epic

      When the traditional shepherd
figure of the pastoral is associated
with other rulers of flocks, like
kings and bishops, then the pastoral
begins to take on the qualities of an
heroic epic.
```

You will typically find yourself making three kinds of notes: a) If who expressed the thought or how it was expressed is important, you will probably quote the passage directly. Be unmistakably legible and accurate, identifying the whole with quotation marks and any omissions with ellipses, recording the exact page number(s) on which the passage appears. b) If the thought is a prevailing opinion or reasonably apparent observation, you will probably paraphrase the passage. Be sure to express the thought in your own words, which means you must do more than change a word here and there. c) If some more or less original thought occurs to you in the process of researching the article — and this is one of the main reasons for reading what others have had to say — jot it down on a note card. Indeed, while many of your ideas will have been incorporated into the outline, and many will later on, the note card is as convenient a way of keeping track of original ideas as it is for recording ideas from your study of primary and secondary sources.

8) *Prepare a working outline of the article and arrange your note cards accordingly.* As a result of your research you will make some changes in the content and order of your outline. Certainly you will add considerably to its length, for the working outline of a professional article is typically more detailed than that for any other prose form. Incorporate the more important notes into the outline and arrange the others according to the outline so they will be readily accessible as you write. You will, of course, be selective — putting aside many notes because they are irrelevant, or superfluous, or duplications, or unconvincing. And you will revise the headings of those note cards you plan to use — making them more specifically descriptive.

9) As you revise the working outline, *keep the traditional parts of the article in mind.* The *Beginning* may contain the following: a) general remarks about the subject, b) the question, or problem and its background — including, perhaps, some reference to other published discussions of the same question and a brief explanation of why still another article on the same subject is necessary, c) the purpose and method, and d)

the answer, or solution—which is, of course, a quick statement of the thesis. But the Beginning is always short, and especially in a short article, the parts are frequently abbreviated and combined in various ways, presented in different order, or implicit enough that they need not be expressed at all.

The following is a reasonably standard beginning paragraph.

> "Oh! To hear him!. . . . To hear the names he's giving me! That Orlick! Oh! Oh!" With these words, Mrs. Joe Gargery reaches the climax of her hysterical fit and Dickens begins a series of violent incidents that seem to bear but an obscure relevance to the plot of *Great Expectations*. A unified reading of the subsequent episodes that develop Mrs. Joe's character might treat her as an extended metaphor or allegory among the many others expressing the theme of the novel. Mrs. Joe's passion for respectability is central to the main theme of *Great Expectations,* because more than any other person she has had the shaping of Pip's conscience, his infantile and perdurable sense of right and wrong. The novel as a whole treats of social injustice and that theme too may also explicate Mrs. Joe's private struggle with her own conscience, for Dickens is apparently very concerned with the conflict between respectable prosperity and shameful poverty in the public scene and with the individual attempt to adapt private values to the status quo.—John Lindberg, "Individual Conscience and Social Injustice in *Great Expectations*."*

The *Middle* consists of the steps in your argument, a series of subordinate assumptions in defense of your thesis with evidence presented in support of each. And the *Ending*, though it may include a summary, is basically a conclusion ending—a restatement of the thesis and discussion of its implications.

The following is a typical ending paragraph:

> Such methods, together with techniques of biological control of insects already in use and under development, could greatly reduce the present reliance on hazardous insecticides. The insects have shown that they cannot be conquered per-

* From *College English*, November, 1961 (Vol. 23, No. 2). Reprinted by permission of the National Council of Teachers of English and the author.

manently by the brand of chemical warfare we have been using up to now. After all, they had become battle-hardened from fighting the insecticide warfare of the plants for more than 100 million years. By learning from the plants and sharpening their natural weapons we should be able to find effective ways of poisoning our insect competitors without poisoning ourselves. — Paul R. Ehrlich and Peter H. Raven, "Butterflies and Plants."*

Once you review your notes, and revise the outline, you are probably ready to write a first draft.

10) *Concentrate on expanding the outline and notes keyed to it into prose with as little deviation from plan as possible.* Elaborate each point in the outline as fully as you can within reason. And follow the outline explicitly. If other ideas or other ways of developing the article occur, by all means consider incorporating them — but make the changes in the outline before writing one, or you will risk losing your sense of direction. Since you will write a better first draft if carried along by the momentum of your enthusiasm, do what you can to keep from becoming bogged down with problems that can be put off until later. Specifically, don't worry over the manner of your expression. It is enough for now that the thought is clearly stated; in later revisions you can see that it is also effectively said. In the case of direct quotations, clip the note card containing the passage to the page. (This also reduces the chance of error through repeated copying.) Footnotes and other documentation can be abbreviated for the time being. (The author's last name and a page number usually suffices.) In order to get the heart of the article written with dispatch, some students prefer not to write the beginning until later, knowing it will be thoroughly revised. Still others prefer to write it first, feeling it gets them off to a good start to have the way clearly pointed out. Experiment to find out which works best for you.

11) You may have hit upon the right *title* before now. But if not, this is a good point at which to begin considering possi-

bilities. Since the title of a scholarly article must, above all, be descriptive, it is most difficult to invent one that is also short and provocative. If you can't come up with an effective conventional title, you might consider one which, in addition to a short, provocative, and reasonably descriptive main title, also incorporates a necessarily longer, less exciting, but more specifically descriptive sub-title.

Here are some suggestions how effective titles might be written: "Two Fossil Floras of the Negev Desert," "*Perkin Warbeck* as 17th Century Psychological Play," "*Blackberry Winter* and the Use of Archetypes," "Fallen from Time: The Mythic Rip Van Winkle," "Madagascar Lemurs: Isolated Primates."

12) *See to it that the article reads smoothly.* In addition to the usual measures taken to refine your expression, you will condense here and expand there (sometimes with the aid of scissors and paste or Scotch tape) in order to achieve the desired clarity and emphasis. And you will pay special attention to the salient parts of the article — the beginning and ending, the transitions at every level, the way the thesis is introduced and developed.

13) You will also *review* (and probably considerably revise) *the manner in which quotations are integrated with the text.* Some badly conceived professional articles appear little more than anthologies of pertinent quotations. To avoid making such an impression — and at the same time use a fair number of quotations, generally your most effective form of evidence — you must not allow them to impede the flow of your prose. It is, for example, much smoother to say,

> Neither the vestiges of puritan pride nor the new-found sense of power over nature can permit man to accept life as "something in one cell that doesn't need to think" or as "merely strange dark interludes in the electrical display of God the Father!"

than it would be to write,

> Neither the vestiges of puritan pride nor the new-found sense of power over nature can permit man to accept life as de-

> scribed by the two major characters in the play. Edmund Darrell decides that "Thinking doesn't matter a damn! Life is something in one cell that doesn't need to think." And later, Nina concludes "Yes, our lives are merely strange dark interludes in the electrical display of God the Father!"

Do not quote at all unless who expressed the thought or how it was expressed is important. Quote from a passage only what is necessary to illustrate your point. Use the ellipsis (to mark omissions) and square brackets (to enclose editorial comment) as a means of abbreviating the passage. There are basically three ways of weaving quotations into the text: a) By holding the quotation down to a phrase or a sentence or two, you will be able to incorporate it into one of your own sentences. b) If because of the length or nature of the quotation this is impossible, you must introduce the quotation in some more obvious way. c) And if it runs to more than three lines, indent and single space the quotation as well.

14) *Documenting* your scholarly article is really not so difficult if you have kept track of where your evidence came from, and if you have reported or quoted it accurately. You must, however, own one or more of the following, not only to answer the questions which are bound to occur in documenting your work, but to find out what professional practice is with regard to manuscript form: *A Manual for the Writers of Term Papers, Theses, and Dissertations* by Kate L. Turabian (Chicago: University of Chicago, 1955); *Form and Style in Thesis Writing* by William G. Campbell (Boston: Houghton Mifflin, 1954); *Literary Scholarship* by James E. Thorpe (Boston: Houghton Mifflin, 1964); *Words into Type* by Marjorie E. Skillin and Robert M. Gay (New York: Appleton-Century-Crofts, 1964); *The MLA Style Sheet* compiled by William R. Parker (obtainable for 50 cents from the Modern Language Association, 6 Washington Place, New York City 10003); and *A Practical Style Guide for Authors and Editors* by Margaret Nicholson (New York: Holt, Rinehart and Winston, 1967). Basic rules are few and simple: You need not document a prevailing opinion or reasonably apparent observation even if it was suggested to you by another writer. You must document any term or idea that is clearly the product of one man's original thought.

And you must document every quotation. In short, you must always acknowledge the source of your information when it is required by courtesy (and by law) and when authoritative opinion or textual evidence is essential in supporting your thesis.

Here is a summary of the way in which notes are usually handled:

—Notes are indicated in the text by a raised (or "superior") number following the reference or quotation; the note itself is identified by a corresponding raised number.

—Whether notes are placed at the bottom of the page—becoming footnotes—and separated from the text by a line (or "rule"), or placed on a separate sheet at the end of the article, as they are most frequently done, they are numbered consecutively throughout the article.

—Ordinarily each quotation is noted, but if several excerpts from the same passage are quoted in the same paragraph of the article, a common note will suffice.

—The most common reference to a book is: The author's name in normal order, followed by a comma; the title of the book, underlined and followed by a comma; the place, publishing company, and date of publication, enclosed in parentheses, the place followed by a colon and the publishing company followed by a comma; and finally the page number(s), followed by a period.

[1] E. G. R. Taylor, *The Haven-Finding Art: A History of Navigation from Odysseus to Captain Cook,* (London: Hollis & Carter, 1958), p. 61.

But many book references are, of necessity, exceptional.

[2] Winston S. Churchill, *The Birth of Britain* (Vol. I of *A History of English Speaking Peoples,* 4 vols.: New York: Dodd, Mead & Company, 1956), 332.

[3] Herodotus, *The Persian Wars,* trans. George Rawlinson (New York: Random House, 1942), p. 595.

[4] William Shakespeare, *The Tragedy of King Lear,* I. v. 56.

— The most common reference to an article is: the author's name in normal order, followed by a comma; the title of the article, enclosed in quotation marks, followed by a comma (before the closing quotation marks!); the name of the periodical, underlined and followed by a comma; the volume number in capital Roman numerals, followed by a comma; the month and the year, enclosed in parentheses, followed by a comma; and finally the page number(s), followed by a period.

> [1] David L. Dineley, "Problematic Conodonts," *Natural History,* LXXII (January, 1963), 21.

But there are exceptions to the usual article references as well.

> [2] "Medicine's Next Decade," *The New York Times,* January 3, 1967, p. 36.
>
> [3] William Sansom, "A Country Walk," in *The Stories of William Sansom* (Boston: Little, Brown and Company, 1963), p. 355.
>
> [4] Newton Chester Whittier, "Squall and Squall Line," *Encyclopedia Britannica* (1965), XXI, 267.

— For subsequent references, the author's last name followed by the page number(s) will normally suffice. (Both *op. cit.* and *loc. cit.* are unnecessary terms and are going out of fashion.) And, of course, if the author's name appears in the text, the page number(s) alone will suffice.

— If in a reasonably short and informal scholarly article you can incorporate some or all of your documentation in the text without impeding its flow, so much the better. If you quote repeatedly from a particular work, subsequent citation after the first note (in which you say in addition to the usual note something to the effect that, "Hereafter all page references to this edition will appear in the body of the text.") need be only a page number in parentheses following the reference.

> Marsden says of himself, "I've never married the word to life!" (p. 624).

Should your article contain only a few references and should you wish to avoid notes altogether, you may present the complete bibliographical information in the text.

> Gwen Benwell and Arthur Waugh, in *Sea Enchantress* (New York: The Citadel Press, 1965, p. 130), explain the representation of a lion suckling a mermaid as "a link with the cult of artemis."

Or an incomplete source note in the text may refer implicitly to the complete facts of publication in the bibliography.

> On page 3 of his informal study of the tropics, *Where Winter Never Comes,* Marston Bates dismisses Huntington's theories about the relationship between civilization and climate as the case of a man who "did not like warm climates" and who "documented his dislike with impressive learning."

And there are other variations of the form for in-text documentation.

There are, in addition to source notes, *explanatory notes* which are more a part of the text than its documentation. Occasionally you will wish to define a term or offer some incidental but pertinent information, to refer your reader to more detailed published discussion of a point, or to call his attention to another part of your article — but to do so in the text would be an intrusion, a violation of proportion. If it is not used to compensate for something having been omitted or presented out of order, the explanatory note is a useful device.

> [1] See Moorhead, *The Fatal Impact* for a more dramatic account of Cook's death.
>
> [2] Oscar Cargill, in *Intellectual America* (New York: Macmillan, 1941), p. 72, comments that *Strange Interlude* is "a dramatized textbook of all the neuroses discoverable by psychoanalysis."
>
> [3] A thousand years later these mooring holes would furnish the best indication of exactly which shores and waterways the Vikings knew.

If your revisions have been thorough and discriminate, you are probably ready to write the final draft of your scholarly article.

15) One of the last things you will do is *prepare a bibliography.* When in a short article the notes are collected at the end, a bibliography is probably not required. But a longer or more formal article is expected to include a bibliography. The bibliography is both a testimony to your own thoroughness and a contribution to scholarship, providing the reader with a list of materials for further study.

Be selective, don't include every written source you know about on the subject or even all those you looked at. Limit your bibliography to those books and articles that were directly useful in your research, ordinarily items which have appeared in source notes. Arrange the bibliography cards alphabetically by the author's last name or, if the work is unsigned, by the first letter in the title (excepting "a," "an," and "the"). And type them pretty much as they appear on the card, neither numbering the entries nor dividing them according to kind.

Ardrey, Robert. *The Territorial Imperative.* New York: Atheneum, 1966.

Churchill, Winston S. *The Birth of Britain.* Vol. I of *A History of English Speaking Peoples.* 4 vols. New York: Dodd, Mead & Company, 1956.

Herodotus. *The Persian Wars.* Trans. George Rawlinson. New York: Random House, 1942.

Koenig, Marie. "Celtic Coins: A New Interpretation," *Archaeology,* XIX (January, 1966), 24–30.

"Medicine's Next Decade." *The New York Times,* January 3, 1967, p. 36.

Sansom, William. "A Country Walk," in *The Stories of William Sansom.* Boston: Little, Brown and Company, 1963, pp. 355–69.

Shakespeare, William. *The Tragedy of King Lear.* "Arden Edition." Cambridge: Harvard University Press, 1952.

Whittier, Newton Chester. "Squall and Squall Line." *Encyclopedia Britannica* (1965), XXI, 267–68.

16) Ordinarily a title page or cover is not required; instructors sometimes appreciate having one or both, editors much prefer neither. In the case of a longer, more formal work you may find it advisable to prepare not only a cover and title page, but a preface, table of contents, list of tables, list of illustrations, notes page, appendix, and bibliography as well. Then is the time to go to an authoritative guide.

To be sure, correctness and accuracy come at the price of tedious attention to detail. But with it goes all the fascination of unravelling a puzzle. And in a world that somewhat limits our personal access to mystery, here is an opportunity for scholarly adventure.

An Exemplary Professional Article

Enter Ahab, Then All: Theatrical Elements in Melville's Fiction

FRED E. H. SCHROEDER

Aficionados are aware that certain chapters of *Moby Dick* are composed like a play script, complete to stage directions, but few seem to have noticed how frequently Herman Melville employs many other theatrical devices (visual and aural effects) at crucial points in his works. Most often the theatrical effects are blended in clusters around dramatic plot-situations, but they can be reasonably classified into three general techniques: the use of the nine-

From the *Dalhousie Review* (Vol. 46, No. 2). Reprinted by permission of the *Dalhousie Review* and the author.

teenth-century "picture-frame" stage; the use of semi-operatic choruses and bombastic speeches; and the use of theatrical sudden disclosures which are intensified by means of carefully contrived visual focal points. Before analyzing examples of these theatrical elements, however, it is of importance to consider the question of whether theatrical effects — practical stage devices — are consistent with Melville's thematic or, if you will, his dramatic purposes.

The very first chapter of *Moby Dick* provides a clue which suggests that for Melville the stage is a metaphor rather than a mere place for acting. Ishmael, having discussed his reasons for going to sea, begins to inquire into his reasons for writing about the last voyage of the *Pequod:* ". . . I cannot tell why it was exactly that those stage managers, the Fates, put me down for this shabby part of a whaling voyage, when others were set down for magnificent parts in high tragedies, and short and easy parts in genteel comedies, and jolly parts in farces. . . . "[1], and he surmises that he was predestined to the voyage. It is evident that what follows is to be a drama, in which the actors are cast and directed by the Fates. But how large is the stage? Melville is hardly attempting to portray all the world. Rather he presents a small complement of men in the narrow confines of a ship, roaming the most deserted areas of the world, cut off from the rest of humanity except for occasional encounters with like men, on like ships, equally confined and limited in their movements. In this novel, Melville does not say any more about the stage on which he will perform his drama.

Forty years later, however, in *Billy Budd,* Melville falls into the same language of the theatre, although he does not compose any portions of this last novel in the manner of a stage script. Here he becomes most intent on explaining how and why a ship is a suitable microcosm for staging his ideas. In the first paragraph of Chapter 14, he says:

> Passion, and passion in its profoundest, is not a thing demanding a palatial stage whereon to play its part. Down among the groundlings, among the beggars and rakers of the garbage, profound passion is enacted. And the circumstances that provoke it, however trivial and mean, are no measure of its power. In the present instance the stage is a scrubbed gun-deck, and one of the external provocations a man-of-war's spilled soup.[2]

Earlier, in Chapter 11, he had stated why human contacts are intensified on shipboard:

> Now there can exist no irritating juxtaposition of dissimilar personalities comparable to that which is possible aboard a great warship fully manned and at sea. There, every day among all ranks almost every man comes into more or less of a contact with almost every other man (p. 35).[3]

By choosing a ship for his stage, Melville solves a problem that confronts every playwright: selecting a setting which will be limited in size, but which will still provide a natural arena for the interplay of the characters. A ship, when once properly provisioned, can exist independently of the rest of the world for months at a time, allowing the drama to be played out without outside human influence. Melville deliberately describes the independence of the *Pequod,* pointing out that it carries enough fresh water to maintain the crew on the Pacific for the greater part of a year. I believe that one reason for this isolation is thematic, reflecting Ahab's deliberate self-exile from humanity and, ultimately, from sophisticated manifestations of God's law. But the ship also provides a dramatically manageable environment for the exhibition of universal problems of good and evil. A desire to narrow the boundaries of action and focus the reader's attention at crucial moments seems to be characteristic of Melville as well as of the theatre. Focusing is one of the most basic stage devices of modern directorial practice, and Melville's methods are remarkably similar to those of the director. Melville had remarkable stage sense and an eye for vivid visual composition, and the way in which he used these abilities enhanced both the actions and themes of *Moby Dick, Billy Budd,* and *Benito Cereno.*

A most conscious passage which deliberately sets the stage is found in Chapter 19 of *Billy Budd.* The captain, having received Claggart's false report, has decided to confront the accuser with the accused: "The measure he determined upon involved a shifting of the scene, a transfer to a place less exposed to observation than the broad quarter-deck" (p. 48). Melville has used terminology which is peculiar to the language of the theatre, "Shifting of the scene." And later, in chapter 22, when the cabin is described, the description reads like the setting of a scene in a play script:

> The court was held in the same cabin where the unfortunate affair had taken place. This cabin, the Commander's, embraced the entire area under the poopdeck. Aft, and on either side, was a small stateroom; the one room temporarily a jail and the other a dead-house, and a yet smaller compartment leaving a space between, expanding forward into a goodly oblong of length coinciding with the ship's beam. A skylight of moderate dimension was overhead, and at each end of the oblong space were two sashed porthole windows . . . (p. 52).

The description is complete to details of the light source and the doors leading offstage; and incidentally, as on stage, we never see the interiors of the offstage rooms. When Billy is closeted in the jail, he is out of sight, and when Captain Vere communicates the decision of the drum-head court to him, "what took place at this interview was never known." In other words, Captain Vere has left by the door "up-right," so to speak, and the audience cannot follow him. This is a convention of the theatre, not of the novel, but Melville has employed it as a means of keeping the focus on the courtroom where the strifeful action is played.

In *Benito Cereno,* Melville also uses the ship as a stage on which a drama is to be played, and he makes use of a more fanciful stage setting than is found in *Billy Budd.* Near the beginning of the narrative as Captain Delano first describes Cereno's ship the *San Dominick,* he speaks of the air of enchantment which a ship met at sea takes on, an enchantment which is a result of its sudden appearance and subsequent disappearance. He says, "The ship seems unreal; these strange costumes, gestures, and faces, but a shadowy tableau just emerged from the deep, which directly must receive back what it gave." An encounter with a ship on the ocean, then, is like a stage play — or a tableau — because the encounter is a limited period within the continuum of time. The ship, like the stage, provides in a neat package a distinct physical and social environment which, so far as an outside observer is concerned, has a beginning and an ending. When the ship pulls away or the curtain falls, the environment of the drama just observed is cut off and the onlooker sees only the neutral sea or the impartial drapery before him.

The *San Dominick,* however, is no mere tableau because Melville prepares the scene in a semi-operatic manner with a droning chorus and percussion orchestra sustaining a weird accompaniment which lasts throughout the greater part of the story. Ranged symmetrically above the bow are four grizzled Negro oakum-pickers who "accompanied their task with a low continuous chant." The other musicians seem to be perched on a stage, for here is how Melville describes the quarter-deck:

> The quarter-deck rose into an ample elevated poop, upon the forward verge of which, lifted, like the oakum-pickers, some eight feet above the general throng, sat along in a row, separated by regular spaces, the cross-legged figures of six other blacks; each with a rusty hatchet in his hand, which . . . he was engaged like a scullion in scouring. . . . Though occasionally the four oakum-pickers would briefly address some person or persons in the crowd below, yet the six hatchet polishers neither spoke to others nor breathed a whisper among themselves, but sat intent upon their task, except at intervals, when, with the peculiar love of negroes of uniting industry with pastime, two-and-two they sideways clashed their hatchets together like cymbals, with a barbarous din (p. 9).

Later in the story, as Don Benito paces behind the line of hatchet polishers and looks at the deck below, Captain Delano, reinforcing the stage viewpoint, sees him as looking "from a stage-box into the pit."

The quarter-deck of the *San Dominick* is so very much like a stage that it seems strange that Melville does not employ raised decks more frequently. The reason that he does not is simply that, even as early as 1799, the year of Captain Delano's story, a deck elevated so high above the main deck was practically an anachronism. Looking at the antiquated ship in the harbour, the captain surmises that it must be a converted treasure ship or a "retired frigate of the Spanish navy" such as were "at intervals encountered along that Main," and he comments that its rigging and design "appeared to have undergone no material change from their original warlike and Froissart pattern." Captain Delano's reference to mediaeval ships (as pictured in Froissart's *Chronicles)* undoubtedly alludes to the high turreted forecastle and after castle, features which had all but disappeared by the mid-seventeenth century.[4] In short, Melville has selected, as a stage for performing his drama, a ship which has been afloat for more than a century. I believe that it would not be unreasonable to suggest that he deliberately set the scene no later than 1799 mainly to utilize this particular kind of "stage" with its peculiarly appropriate stage effects: the ornate scrollwork and gilding of the old warship effectively intensify Spanish decadence and place Benito Cereno's apparent weakness of character in ironic contrast to the symbols of past glory. That comparing the fading grandeur of Spain to Cereno's degradation was one of Melville's methods is made clear when Delano watches Don Benito being shaved and notices that the royal banner of Spain is being used as a barber's sheet. The effects are contrived, but as will be seen in *Moby Dick,* Melville would go to great lengths to achieve a single visual dramatic effect.

Chapter 99, "The Doubloon," one of the most contrived scenes of theatrical staging in *Moby Dick,* for example, is significantly enough one of the most important portions of the book, summarizing the attitudes and prejudices of seven major characters. The doubloon has been nailed to the mast for most of the voyage and it had been a focal point for the crew when nailed up. Now it is a focal point again, but this time it is not the centre of histrionic action, but is rather the object of successive soliloquies. As each man goes to the coin, he is observed by the others, hidden about the ship like so many characters in a Shakespeare comedy or a Mozart opera. Each comes forward, speaks his peculiar thoughts in his own peculiar idiom, and retires to observe the next man. If we discount Ishmael's opening description — although it is written in his own bookish mode of speech — we notice another excellent piece of stage writing: Ahab, in his soliloquy, describes the imprint of the coin in detail, thereby communicating the details of its appearance to the audience, who naturally were not able to see its design. By the time we come to the last observer, poor mad Pip, we are told that the doubloon, this focal point, is "the ship's navel," the focus of sinful greed.

The presentation of this chapter is essentially theatrical — no novelist need crowd a scene unnaturally with seven people to provide seven different attitudes toward one symbol. Hawthorne, for example, used the same device of commenting on a visual image in *The Scarlet Letter,* when at dawn, a cloud shaped like an "A" catches the ruddy morning light. His approach, however, was to take the novelist's license to enter different homes, different rooms, different minds, to evoke a variety of interpretations of the vision. It should be noticed particularly that Hawthorne relates the unspoken thoughts of the viewers. But Melville, in his theatrical style, has each character speak aloud. The soliloquy, in fact, is one of the most characteristic methods in *Moby Dick,* and although — as is so strongly manifested in Chapter 99 — Melville can make amazing distinctions between the speech idioms of his characters, none of them speaks a true vernacular. Rather, they all speak the language of the stage and the pulpit. Even Flask, the very essence of cold practicality, speaks metaphorically. He begins, "I see nothing here, but a round thing made of gold . . . ." (p. 463); but in two lines, this round thing embodies his values. It is for him "nine hundred and sixty cigars."

Another remarkable thing about the language is that it reads well aloud. It soon becomes apparent that one of the reasons for this is that the characters frequently break into regular metre. The following two passages from the Starbuck-Ahab dialogues in Chapter 132, "The Symphony," illustrate the rhythms of their theatrically unrealistic speech:

> "Oh, Starbuck! it is a mild, mild wind, and a mild looking sky. On such a day — very much such sweetness as this — I struck my first whale. . . .
>
> Oh, my Captain, my Captain! grand old heart, after all! . . . Wife and child, too, are Starbuck's — wife and child of his brotherly, sisterly, play-fellow youth. . . ." (pp. 580–581).

There are few actors who could resist reproducing the thick essence of a balmy wind in "very much such sweetness as this," or the metrical heaping of images of home and family bonds in Starbuck's "brotherly, sisterly, play-fellow youth." It is not only that the poetic language suggests the stage — most novelists indulge in some rhapsody, although ordinarily as narrators — but that the diction is often on the verge of bombast. It is the language of the theatre.

Melville has a way of saving reference to some of the symbols until they can be produced suddenly in a brilliant dramatic flourish, and the symbols are invariably large enough to be easily seen — sometimes seeming obvious to the point of crudity. An outstanding example of this is found in Chapter 100 of *Moby Dick,* "Leg and Arm." Ahab calls to the *Samuel Enderby:*

> "Hast seen the White Whale!"
> "See you this?" and withdrawing it from the fold that had hidden it, he held up a white arm of Sperm whale bone, terminating in a wooden head like a mallet (p. 466).

Then follows the meeting of the two maimed captains, in an almost embarrassingly dramatic act. Ahab is hoisted to the *Samuel Enderby*. We are told that this is done because Ahab could not manipulate the ladder. This is undoubtedly true. But it is also done to set up the stage for a symbolic action which would be ridiculous if Ahab were not slung aloft:

> With his ivory arm frankly thrust forth in welcome, the other captain advanced, and Ahab, putting out his ivory leg, crossing the ivory arm (like two swordfish blades) cried out in his walrus way "Aye, aye, hearty! let us shake bones together! — an arm and a leg! — an arm that can never shrink, d'ye see; and a leg that can never run" (p. 467).

I think that most novelists would assume that a thrilling and darkly significant effect was produced by the other captain's sudden revelation of his arm; but a dramatist is compelled to illustrate visually important relationships which may be apparent only in the mind of one character, and Melville, whether consciously or unconsciously writing in the theatrical mode, has therefore prepared elaborate machinery to cross the ivory limbs.

The same type of theatrical sudden disclosure occurs frequently in *Moby Dick*. Queequeg's "ramadan" in Chapter 17 is revealed by having Ishmael shoulder the door down from a running start; at the close of Chapter 47, Ahab's devilish yellow boat-crew spills forth from below decks as the remainder of the crew stands transfixed; and in Chapter 131, after the *Pequod* has encountered the *Delight* just as it is burying another of Moby Dick's victims, it turns suddenly away:

> As Ahab now glided from the dejected *Delight*, the strange life-buoy hanging at the *Pequod*'s stern came into conspicuous relief.
> "Ha! Yonder! look yonder, men!" cried a foreboding voice in her wake. "In vain, oh, ye strangers, ye fly our sad burial; yet but turn us your taffrail to show us your coffin!" (p. 578).

In a similar situation, in *Benito Cereno*, just after it is suddenly revealed to Captain Delano that Cereno is not the persecutor but the persecuted, another stage-like sudden revelation places Delano's reversal of attitude in brilliant relief as the sub-stage curtain is suddenly lifted to reveal the figurehead:

> But by this time, the cable of the *San Dominick* has been cut; and the fag-end, in lashing out, whipped away the canvas shroud about the beak, suddenly revealing, the bleached hull swung round toward the open ocean, death for the figurehead, in a human skeleton; chalky comment on the chalked words below, "Follow your leader." (pp. 79–80).

And, in *Billy Budd,* there is another such example, as Billy is hanged:

> At the same moment it chanced that the vapory fleece hanging low in the East, was shot through with a soft glory as of the fleece of the Lamb of God seen in mystical vision and simultaneously therewith, watched by the wedged mass of upturned faces, Billy ascended; and ascending, took the full rose of the dawn (p. 62).

This scene is one of perfect stage composition: the faces are all directed toward a single figure who is above all the others, and he is singled out to receive weird lighting effect.

There are in *Moby Dick* twelve chapters which employ stage directions. Two blocks of such chapters occur: the first block, Chapters 36 to 40, including the scenes in which Ahab swears his men to his mission; the second, Chapters 119–122, being the scenes of the great storm which demagnetizes the compass. Three isolated chapters have stage directions as well: Chapter 108 with Ahab and the carpenter, and Chapters 127 and 129 with Ahab and Pip. The mere listing of these chapters reveals two important points: Melville seems to use the playwright's method at exceedingly crucial moments, and he uses this method at moments when dialogue and a few elemental motions are needed to develop the basic action. (Obviously the pursuit of the White Whale, while crucial, is all action, and the narrative method is better suited to it.)

The first block of scenes is the finest, starting with words which are as memorable as "Call me Ishmael": "enter Ahab: Then, all"; and building up to a frenzied scene representative of all mankind dancing and singing to the steady beat of the tambourine. The rhythmic background commences in the second paragraph — "Soon his steady, ivory stride was heard . . ." — and leads into the catechism of the sailors:

> "What do ye do when you see a whale, men?"
> "Sing out for him!" . . .
> "And what do ye do next, men?"
> "Lower away, and after him!"
> "And what tune is it ye pull to, Men?"
> "A dead whale or a stove boat!" (p. 171).

And the excitement builds up, interrupted only by Starbuck, until Ahab has his harpooners drink a pact with him from the hollows of their harpoon heads. This chapter is followed by three short chapters, each a soliloquy of a major figure. Here are the stage directions which open each of the chapters:

> *Sunset:* The cabin; by the stern windows; Ahab sitting alone, and gazing out.
> *Dusk:* By the Mainmast; Starbuck leaning against it.
> *First Night Watch:* Stubb solus, and mending a brace.

The very positions of the three men are carefully selected to reflect their characters, before each speaks. Stern Ahab, alone, at the stern windows; Starbuck in a position of anguish, but not standing alone — rather leaning against the mainmast. His first words show that he has relinquished his power to stand independently: "My soul is more than matched; she's over-manned; and by a madman!" And Stubb is disclosed, at work, totally business-like, but understanding in a shallow way, Starbuck's problem:

> ". . . who calls? Mr. Starbuck? Aye, aye, sir — (Aside) he's my superior, he has his too, if I'm not mistaken . . ." (p. 182).

The first block culminates in Chapter 40, which is a play script opening with the stage direction to "raise the foresail" and carrying the men from song to dance, to contemplation of the sea as a sensuous woman, to a quarrel — until all breaks up as nature provides a squall to top the petty squalling of the men. In these scenes, then, we see the welding of the crew into a weapon of vengeance, and the stage-dialogue method has effectively portrayed the wildness and enthusiasm of the moment, while the musical accompaniment provides a steadiness in the background that, contrasting with the headlong drunkenness of the men's speech, creates a tension which probably reflects the tension that is felt on an intellectual plane by Starbuck and Ishmael. This method of producing tension is extremely powerful in the operatic tradition (consider virtually any Verdi opera) and, as we have seen, was used again by Melville in *Benito Cereno* where the inexorable droning of the oakum-pickers is punctuated by the clashing of the hatchet-cymbals, which provides a rigid regularity in tense contrast with Captain Delano's vacillating thoughts about Don Benito and his crew.

This fortieth chapter of *Moby Dick* is the most theatrical: never again does Melville bring the whole crew into the action as a chorus, and he uses only a few crew members other than the harpooners as single characters. But when he does, he returns to the stage technique. When lightning strikes the ship and all the crew gather around aghast, Ahab steals the show, posing before the "trinity of Flames". Finally, when Ahab does speak to crew members — the carpenter and the cabin boy — Melville also reverts to dramatic dialogue.

One is tempted to suggest that Melville meant *Moby Dick* to be a drama, but that the narrative of Ishmael, the digressions on cetology, and the violent action of the actual whale-hunts are too essential and could be dealt with only in the novel form. Melville did, however, make conscious use of theatrical conventions, probably to reinforce his view of a ship as a stage; as much of a microcosm as a stage, and yet as limited as a stage. He undoubtedly anticipated modern playwrights in accepting the limitations of a small physical environment, and in fact turned the limitations to his advantage by intensifying human contacts and intellectual problems through the use of highly selective and vivid symbols, placed in visual prominence. His dialogue is artificial, yet each actor has his characteristic mode of speech, usually established by means of distinctive metaphors. In short, the peculiar stage passages in *Moby Dick* enhance the narration, and support the ship-stage attitude which Melville expressed most fully in *Billy Budd*.

NOTES

1. *Moby Dick; or, The Whale* (New York: Heritage Press, 1943), p. 7.
2. *Billy Budd*, in *American Short Novels*, ed. R. P. Blackmur (New York: Crowell, 1960), p. 38.
3. *Benito Cereno*, in *Shorter Novels of Herman Melville* (New York: Horace Liveright, 1928), p. 8.
4. An illustrated translation of Froissart appeared in New York in 1854, two years before the publication of *Benito Cereno*. Eighteenth-century architectural draw-

ings in Chapman's *Architectura Navalis Mercatoria 1768,* Neu Herausgegeben von Robert Loef (Berlin, 1930) indicate that the ship decks in 1768 were flat, and that even frigates were not built with a rear deck elevated more than five feet. Judging from illustrations in *Navires et Marins* (Paris, 1946), Volume II, in the section "Les Trois-Mats du Commerce", pp. 138–144, the *San Dominick* may have been built before 1679.

An Analysis

1) Assuming the *Dalhousie Review* is typical of scholarly reviews, quarterlies, journals — what sort of person would be most likely to encounter an article such as this? Could only scholars, "aficionados" as the author termed them, read "Enter Ahab, Then All" with any enthusiasm?
2) What is the subject of the article? Does the title and the sub-title, the first sentence make this instantly clear?
3) How would you reply to a reader of the article whose response upon reading it was a bored "So what"? On what grounds could you justify the effort expended by Fred E. H. Schroeder, not to mention that of his readers, upon pure scholarship of this sort?
4) Is the thesis of "Enter Ahab, Then All" an utterly new and original insight? If basically the same thought has already occurred to many of the Melville aficionados who will read this article, as Schroeder suggests in sentence one, what justification does he present for writing another article on the subject in sentence two?
5) How many times is the thesis stated? What is the specific reason for each expression of the thesis?
6) Why was the article given both a title and a subtitle?
7) For what kind of statement does the author occasionally lapse into first person? Is it a subtle means for separating factual observation from personal opinion? Do these infrequent direct addresses to the reader reveal anything of the writer's personality? Or does he remain always the disinterested scholar?
8) Could you have written this article? How would you have prepared yourself for writing such an article or something like it?

9) How would you describe the general form of the article?
10) Is there a clear beginning, middle, and end?
11) Are the various parts of the beginning — general remarks, the problem and its background, the purpose and method, the thesis — effectively presented? (In so short an article they are likely to be abbreviated and combined in some way.)
12) Could you outline the main topics of the middle? Are they reasonably distinct and yet clearly subordinate assumptions leading to the expression of the same thesis? What is the relative emphasis of each topic? How is the relation of one topic to the next and to the overall purpose maintained?
13) What kind of evidence does the author present in support of his ideas? Is each expression of an idea supported by evidence? Is the kind and quantity of evidence always completely adequate?
14) Describe what the author does in the ending. Has he made his point and effectively stated it once again?
15) How would you describe Fred E. H. Schroeder's prose style in "Enter Ahab, Then All"? Dull and pretentious? Or lively, modest, and natural?

Assignments

1) Make a study of a work of fiction, poetry, or drama; decide what aspect you wish to treat; and formulate a thesis. Write a short professional article (500–1000 words, which many journals would refer to as a "note") in support of your thesis, drawing exclusively upon the primary source for evidence.
2) Using a mixture of primary and secondary sources, write a short professional article (1000–1500 words) on a person or event of historical significance. You may wish to choose a subject of local significance, for which you will have to do a certain amount of especially imaginative research.
3) Using secondary sources almost exclusively, i.e. newspaper and magazine stories, radio and television reports, make a

study of some current and controversial event. Compare and weigh the evidence. Write a short but fully documented account which represents for you the truth. How did you evaluate the secondary sources?

4) Make a schematic analysis of a short published professional article, identifying the beginning, the middle and the ending with marginal brackets; circling each clear statement of the thesis; underlining each subordinate assumption; and, if it is appropriate, placing a "p" or "s" by each piece of evidence according to whether it is primary or secondary.

5) In three divergent scholarly or technical articles, estimate the proportion of primary and secondary source evidence. What influence does the nature of the subject seem to have upon the resulting ratios or percentages? Might the authors have used a higher proportion of primary sources to good advantage? What efforts did they make to choose the most pertinent and persuasive secondary sources?

6) Compile a bibliography for a specific topic. Be exhaustive but selective. Compare your list with those prepared by your colleagues for the same topic. How closely do they compare? How does yours compare with the best?

7) Retrace the steps followed by a writer in researching and supplying evidence for a professional article by running down every source footnote and every bibliographical entry. Has he exploited his sources well? Can you find other readily available sources which he apparently did not consult that would have been even more useful? Using the same sources as he, could you write an article on another aspect of the same subject?

8) Find two professional articles (on the same general subject if possible), one marred by a somewhat self-consciously pretentious style and the other written more naturally. From your study of these two articles, do you think it possible to be learned and precise without using technical jargon and pedantic expressions? Or do you think the dangers of overstatement and impressionistic writing are greater?

9) Rewrite a popular article as a professional article. Among other changes, you will have to limit the subject further, supply more and different kinds of evidence, document your sources, employ a more cautious and explicit style. Compare the results.

10) Now, in view of what you have learned about the professional article, write such a prose form following as nearly as possible the described procedure.

4

The Personal Essay

The essay, not so pointedly factual or instructive as the article, but more ranging and speculative, is written for a reader of philosophical interests and urbane tastes. Of all prose forms it is the most literary, for whether the writer chooses to reveal anything of himself directly or subordinate the man to the occasion, the essay is written with an art that far surpasses that of ordinary published communication. Perhaps, as we are told, the mood of the age is not right for the essay, but a great many readers find it the best of all possible forms: the *personal essay* possessing the intimacy of a private conversation and the reflective beauty of a lyric; the *formal essay* recalling the wise and prophetic dignity of a classical oration. The customary and quite real distinction between the two general types of essays is an indication of its diversity and adaptability. Indeed, the essayical spirit is not likely to diminish.

The Personal Essay as a Form

Any description of the personal essay must include these qualities: the personal element, the suggestive treatment of the subject, the informal structure, the graceful and effortless style, and the literary effect.

The *personal element* is naturally a major attribute of the form. The personal essay is a fragment of autobiography, for it is inevitably self-revealing. The tastes and impressions and experiences of a unique individual dominate the essay to such an extent that it simply could not have been written by anyone else. Yet it is not autobiographical in the most limited sense. It is personal but not private. What the writer does is express an individual view of a universal subject. That is, he objectifies subjective experience.

The reader's impression is of having broken in on a personal reverie. The essay has also been compared to a lyric poem. But it is more like a dialogue or, better, a quiet conversation with a friend; for it is in every way one writer speaking with one reader, man to man, as perfect equals. The persona, or speaker, may be any kind of personality. But generally he is sincere, modest, frank, curious, observant, calm, affable, fanciful. Even though the essay may have been provoked by something about which he is mildly discontent, the writer never loses his sense of humor. And his manner is always intimate and confidential, never pompous or distant, never platitudinous or cliché ridden.

In a form so dominated by the spirit and whims of the writer, a *suggestive treatment of the subject is inevitable.* The subject itself is often of no great consequence and may appear trifling. This is because the essayist's vision is miniature, focused on the little things and commonplaces (but not the silly, the ephemeral), fit subjects for reflection or reminiscence. Even if the subject is of apparent significance, his treatment will in no way be a complete and comprehensive statement. This isn't to say the personal essay is uninformed or frivolous; actually it reveals in a casual way an intimate knowledge of the subject. And it may well be that the really significant subjects in life are quite beyond formal explanation. Certainly the writer of personal essays will not describe, analyze, and evaluate a subject in a very methodical way. Moreover, since the essayist's view is comic — that is, detached, skeptical, amused by the human scene — his treatment of any subject is apt to be light, whimsical, humorous. In this respect at least, though he may be deadly in earnest, he does not take anything very seriously.

The subject receives this treatment partly because of the *informal structure* of the personal essay. It is simply too brief and tentative a form to permit elaborate schemes of order and organization. Actually both are present, but the basis is more psychological than logical. The essayist depends more on the subtle devices of momentum and on simple association than on more obvious and closely reasoned schemes. The personal essay is more digressive and allusive than deliberate and explicit, more descriptive and narrative than expository or argumentative. Indeed, the most definite thing you can say about the structure of the personal essay is that it brings considerable knowledge to bear on a specific subject, that it has a definite point (or thesis) and a climax, and that it does have a beginning and middle and end. Despite the apparent lack of any itinerary, the personal essay always seems to get where it's going with surprising zip — suggesting that here at least, the shortest distance between two points is not a straight line.

The informal structure is matched by a *graceful and effortless style*. The personal essay could not, of course, be what it is without employing a style that is informal, sometimes colloquial, easy and relaxed conversational, natural, spontaneous, even impetuous. But style is finally a personal affair, the distinctive idiom of this writer on this occasion. The personal essay is written with style, with a manner of expression that is never perfunctory, never simply correct, always preeminently expressive.

But whatever else it is or is not, the personal essay is *literary*. Its knowledge reflects a well-read and speculative mind; its allusions, wit, irony, satire evince a nimble intellect; its images, metaphors, symbols suggest a keen observer and lively imagination; its sounds and rhythms, appropriate always if not euphonic, are proof of a lyric sense. In the personal essay the fusion of form and content is particularly right; the means becomes the end. In short, this spectacle of a civilized man describing the good life (perhaps lamenting its passing or yearning for its attainment) is intensely literary.

Something very like the modern personal essay was undoubtedly written in antiquity, but the recent history of the form is brief. Upon his retirement from active life in the late sixteenth century, the French philosopher Montaigne became a writer of what he called "essais" — brief and tentative discussions of most anything that would interest a curious and contemplative mind, "idleness," "liars," "smells and odors," "cannibals," "sleeping," "some verses of Vergil's." Derived as it was from a popular French literary form, the *leçon morale* (a collection of wise sayings on a particular subject), the essay was from the beginning, somewhat moral and aphoristic. And since Montaigne, like many a humanist, considered his own thoughts to be representative of those shared by other thoughtful men, the informal essay possessed from the beginning that distinctive personal element as well. Although it has been modified a good deal, the contemporary essay clearly bears the marks of Montaigne and of the light and gracious Gallic Temperament generally.

The first essayist in English, writing a few years after Montaigne but also in the sixteenth century, was the British statesman-scientist, Francis Bacon. Although he appropriated and Anglicized the title, Bacon's essays are more like the sagacious personal reflections of several classical writers, notably Seneca. There is something a little cold-blooded in the way he handles such subjects as "love" and "marriage," and he hasn't much sense of humor, but Bacon's essays are nevertheless quite readable and, indeed, are still read. Bacon's "Of Truth," "Of Death," "Of Marriage and Single Life," "Of Love," "Of Great Places," "Of Travel," "Of Studies," are among the greatest English essays. They are clear, succinct, allusive, aphoristic; you would learn a good deal about one kind of essay by studying them. Since Bacon was an eminently practical man, however, his essays are for the most part advice for getting ahead — hardly in the proper reflective and idealistic tradition of the personal essay.

The informal essay was throughout the seventeenth century a favorite form of the gentlemen writers — Sir William Temple, Abraham Cowley, Sir Thomas Browne, Ben Jonson, Izaak Walton. Except perhaps for the "character," a witty description of a personality type like those written by Sir Thomas Overbury and John Earle, the essayists were content to follow rather explicitly the form established by Montaigne and Bacon. But the sheer popularity of the essay assured its permanence as a literary type. And doubtless some of the sophistication and sensibility of the modern personal essay is attributable to these writers.

In the eighteenth century the personal essay became a truly fashionable form, largely because it was ideally suited to the periodical — a publication of several pages appearing at irregular intervals and dealing with subjects of timely interest, the forerunner of both the newspaper and magazine. Virtually all the best writers of the day — Daniel Defoe, Richard Steele, Joseph Addison, Jonathan Swift, Alexander Pope, Samuel Johnson, Lord Chesterfield, Horace Walpole, Oliver Goldsmith — tried their hand at writing essays. And the large, new middle-class audience read them with zeal. The essay began to change, becoming shorter, less introspective, more informal, hence not so learned or aphoristic as before. The wit, irony, satire, and humor we find so appealing in the true personal essay began to develop. In some ways the eighteenth-century essayists were more imaginative than those of our own century, at least when it came to such paraphernalia as imaginary characters, clubs, correspondents. At any rate, readers began to have more leisure and a greater inclination to reflect on their tastes and manners and institutions — and the essay fared very well.

The nineteenth-century audience, and especially the Victorian reader, was much attracted by the personal essay. The same moral earnestness and anxiety to be educated which made this a great age for the formal essay was leavened enough by sentiment and humor to make it a good one for the personal essay as well. The essay of the century before, largely under Addison's influence, was inclined to be preoccupied with the well-worn (marriage, death, friendship) and the ephemeral (coffee houses, dueling, women's fashions), and to deal with these topics in a stereotyped, superficial way. With the rise of Romantic individualism and the increase in the number and size of periodicals, the old Bacon-Addison mold was broken. The personal essay became for the first time truly "personal," that is, intimate and autobiographical, lighter and more literary, less like a learned exercise or belletristic performance. Many of the great nineteenth-century English essays and essayists are familiar — William Hazlitt's "The Fight," Thomas De Quincey's "On the Knocking at the Gate in *Macbeth*," Charles Lamb's "Old China," Charles Dickens's "Noble Savage," William Thackeray's "On University Snobs," Robert Lewis Stevenson's "Pulvis Et Umbra." And even better known are the works of numerous American essayists — Washington Irving's "Traits of Indian Character," Nathaniel Hawthorne's "Old Manse," Henry David Thoreau's *Walden*, Oliver Wendell Holmes's *Autocrat of the Breakfast Table*, Ralph Waldo Emerson's "On Self-Reliance," Mark Twain's "How to Tell a Story."

In the present century the personal essay has, we are told, declined. To be sure, the magazines that publish personal essays are fewer than before, and publishers do not bring out as many collections of essays as they once did. Doubtless there is some truth in the common explanation, that our frenzied age is not right for the calm reflections or low-keyed art of the personal essay. But what of the great essayists of these last sixty or seventy years? G. K. Chesterton, Max Beerbohm, D. H. Lawrence, Virginia Woolf, Aldous Huxley, E. M. Forster, George Orwell; and the Americans H. L. Mencken, James Thurber, E. B. White, Loren Eisely, Joseph Wood Krutch. The personal essay seems likely to survive as long as there are civilized readers. Indeed, the personal essay may, because of its own preeminent sanity, be a means of that survival.

How to Write the Personal Essay

Since you are assuming many of the literary prerogatives of the poet and short story writer, you must use their methods in writing the personal essay — and their methods are not the deliberate ways of the scholar and journalist. The creative process is, of course, largely a unique and private affair, especially that of the essayist; for his is in many ways the most subjective of literary forms. But most writers for most of their essays seem to follow this plan or something like it:

1) *Begin with some abstract thought associated with concrete things or specific events* to such an extent that the things and events stand (or can be made to stand) as metaphors for the thought. Sometimes the thought will come first, sometimes the sensory experience. But in either case, the thought should be a personal sentiment, one which has its origin in mild discontent and one that speaks to the reader's condition; and the things and events should involve a considerable quantity of the solid, perceptible stuff of life.

There is certainly no scarcity of ideas for essays. If you are lucky, you may come upon the germ of an essay quite by accident; you may even be surprised to discover that it has already begun to develop. But most of the time you will have to go looking. And the place to look is rarely among facts, for the personal essay is not a scientific or inductive effort, but a speculative and far-ranging one. Indeed, much of the time you will find yourself looking inward at how a thing strikes you, or at what connection it has with something else you once encountered. Remember, an essayist is first a curious and observant and meditative man — hence, he is always on the look-out for the subject matter, whether the essays get written or not. (You can always stimulate this idea-getting process by asking yourself two questions: What have I just experienced? observed? How do I feel about it now that I've had time to reflect?)

Suppose, for example, that in the course of reading some rather bad verse by a minor poet you came upon these surprisingly memorable lines,

> Red o'er the forest peers the setting sun.
> The line of yellow light dies fast away
> That crowned the eastern copse: and chill and dun
> Falls on the moor the brief November day . . .
>
> John Keble, "Christian Year"

You might well be struck by the realization that our ideas about not only art but life are based overmuch upon total effect, that we have too little appreciation of the part. The thought that fragments and ruins possess a beauty often surpassing that of the whole and perfect (and sometimes even imperfect) original is exactly the sort of thing about which essays are written.

2) Next *summon up and inventory all the relevancies from your experience and observation, reflection and reading.* Begin to build a reservoir of images, metaphors, symbols, allusions, quotations, etc. from which to draw for this essay. Jot them down as they come to you by association — this may be more or less the order that you will mention them in the essay itself. For example, a day of high-piled motionless clouds heaped against the blue might expectedly remind you of a voyage on which you once saw such a sky, of Constable's cloudscapes and Ruskin's descriptions of the great cumulus, of threading the vast canyons between thunderheads in an airplane, of Aristophane's "Clouds."

3) *Add to that reservoir of materials, if necessary, by doing some reading.* You will probably have to check on the accuracy and relevancy of quotations, allusions, details. Run down the exact phrasing of Frome's remark to the effect that great societies worship people and use things while we in America worship things and use people; look to be certain that Gilbert White is, indeed, considered the first field naturalist; find out that those handsome gold-hackled and russet-barred chickens, the kind old masters scattered around the feet of milkmaids, were in fact golden campines.

4) *Decide what your response will be toward the matter of the essay.* A certain consistency of response, especially in those essays where subject and thesis are neither very definite, is basic to the unity of the essay. You will probably need to establish in your own mind the persona, the "speaker" in this personal essay. You may even choose to jot down a brief character sketch of this persona, whether or not it is you speaking — and, of course, you may well decide to assume for this essay a role other than the one in which you normally confront life. You might, for example, choose for the moment to be someone else — a cultured, bookish, traveled, middle-aged bachelor who has just thrown over his New York job to go live in the country — in order to make a kind of observation about life that you cannot as Sally, age nineteen, student at Midwestern U., cheer-

leader and rush chairman, even though Sally is quite capable of making valid and even profound statements while being herself. At the very least you will have to decide whether you will be whimsical and playful, or methodical and dignified, or some other frame of mind.

5) *Decide whether your essay is to have a narrative or descriptive center.* Although we speak of it as an expository form, the personal essay often begins by relating a story or painting a word picture, or contains details which to all purposes does one or the other. And it may be based almost exclusively on a narrative or descriptive framework. Obviously, anything dynamic, anything which moves in space and time, whether it is a story or a natural process, invites narrative treatment; and anything static, which is relatively motionless, like an object or a scene, seems to demand a descriptive approach. It may be best, however, to shift away from what appears, because of the nature of the subject, to be the inevitable choice. The writer has the right and in almost every case can exercise it without distorting the subject. Often you will shift from a descriptive to a narrative treatment — as Homer does in the *Iliad* when he "describes" Achilles' armor by narrating the way in which it was forged and worked.

6) Only now are you ready to *put aside random speculations and begin thinking in terms of a specific subject and thesis.* Your essay will, no doubt, touch on many things, but in the end it will be clear that even the apparent digressions and irrelevancies all have some bearing on a single subject. And in almost every essay you write, the purpose, or central thought of the essay is summed up at least once. Some personal essays are more pointed than others. Most give the impression of being more unpremeditated and rambling than they actually are. But even in the freest, you are on safer ground if you provide your reader with a clear sense of what the essay is about and to what object it is written. And not only is a clear subject-and-thesis desirable, but the subject-and-thesis must be something you can handle in the brief and casual personal essay. You will, in fact, do better with a limited subject than with a broad subject. Your major problem will always lie, not in a lack of knowledge about your subject, but in your failure to

present what knowledge you have in an effective way. So while the personal essay is in some respects far-ranging, it is largely addressed to a specific subject-and-thesis — even though both subject and thesis may be suggestively developed. For example, George Orwell's "Some Thoughts On the Common Toad," has as its apparent subject the phenomena of spring, especially mating toads; the essay is in truth a form of social criticism developing the thesis that

> by retaining one's childhood love of such things as trees, fishes, butterflies and . . . toads, one makes a peaceful and decent future a little more probable, and that by preaching the doctrine that nothing is to be admired except steel and concrete, one merely makes it a little surer that human beings will have no outlet for their surplus energy except in hatred and leader-worship.*

7) *Jot down a list of topics for the essay in about the order you plan to use them.* Don't be concerned about phrasing and don't be too detailed. Keep thinking of these notes as tentative. And try out one scheme and then another until you find the most promising. From this point form will be a major consideration. Look first at what design the material seems to call for. Then, within the confines of this design, try to order your materials most effectively. In brief, what you want here are from three to seven topics; providing for a beginning, middle, and end; with topics of the middle part, regardless what other schemes may be used, ordered in terms of increasing relevance and importance; planning for something strong to occur toward the end of the essay. A personal essay on old maps, for example, might be written around these topics:

— Beginning: Thesis — the disappearance of vast white spaces, of *terra incognita* from maps of the world has cramped the fancy — for the imagination is most stirred by the vaguely dreamed of and the wholly unknown.

— Modern maps, in their detail and exactness and, above all, in their practical uses, are dull affairs.

— Old maps with their showy hues and designs are the most romantic expression of the imaginative spirit.

— The only unknown seas and lands remain in literature.

— But even modern writers only thinly disguise familiar places.

— Ending: In the blank spaces of old maps and in the make-believe lands of childhood there was space for dreaming that has quite gone out with the accurate charting of the world.

8) *Incorporate the minor details.* Don't work out a complete and explicit formal outline, the object is only to have the materials for writing conveniently at hand. You may want to revise and certainly you will have to enlarge the brief "outline" you jotted down earlier, deciding what you can and can't use in this essay. This will be determined largely by the conception of form that has begun to emerge.

9) *Consider first the ideas*—especially the main point of the essay. And begin to indicate, in this draft, the particular attitude you have chosen to maintain in presenting your material. If you have decided to be humorous or ironic, you can —even in this draft—begin to create the phrases and locutions that will reveal to your reader that "this is for fun" or "this means something other than what it actually says." If you choose to be humorous, you will use such well-established devices of humor as *exaggeration, surprise,* and *dehumanization.* If you choose to be ironic, you will use the standard devices of *inversion with exaggeration* ("The novel was brilliant" for "The novel was quite bad"), *negation* ("The novel was not bad" for "The novel was bad"), and *understatement* ("The novel was not very good" for "The novel was terrible").

10) Next, *attend to form.* Your essay should have the basic design of "beginning, middle, end," and that properly proportioned. You may need to elaborate and expand here, eliminate or condense there, in order to control proportion and empha-

sis. Though your personal essay can't do without a *beginning,* you may introduce your subject matter — the main task of any beginning — in a more casual and indirect way than would be possible in other forms of writing. You can construct a delayed beginning, not stating your subject in the first sentence of the first paragraph as you would normally do, but presenting the subject at the end of the first paragraph or even somewhere in the second paragraph. The delayed beginning is appropriate to the personal essay because it helps create the light and casual tone, and suggests that the author is willing to spend a little time in setting the stage for his subject. The delayed beginning of E. M. Forster's "My Wood," although brief, is so independent of the essay proper that it virtually constitutes a prologue:

> A few years ago I wrote a book which dealt in part with the difficulties of the English in India. Feeling that they would have no difficulties in India themselves, the Americans read the book freely. The more they read it the better it made them feel, and a cheque to the author was the result. I bought a wood with the check. . . . [The subject of the essay is the effect of property, the wood, upon character.] *

11) In the *middle section be sure that your essay has an apparent and appropriate design, and enough continuity and momentum* that the reader will move from one thought to the next smoothly and swiftly. Notice the apparent design and the transitional devices in these first lines from the major paragraphs in J. B. Priestley's "On Education":

> When I was sixteen I left school and found myself a job in a wool office. . . .
>
> Looking back, I can see quite clearly now that the great formative period for me was neither school nor the Cambridge years. It was 1911–14, when nobody was trying to educate me nor paying for me to be instructed, when, in fact, I was working (though as little as possible) in the wool office. . . .

> The truth is, I was fortunate during those years in my environment. . . .
>
> Let us take a look at what seem at first to be more formal processes of education. . . .
>
> Now we have to spend so much on the school that we cannot afford to educate the street. . . .
>
> But no, I must not growl and grumble. I will simply state the case, as I see it. I owe most to a time when I was not being formally educated but when I enjoyed an environment favourable to a youth of my sort. . . .*

12) Whether the *ending* is a quick summary or a conclusion, it should come full circle by renaming the subject and referring once again to the matter of the beginning. The only exception to this rule is the occasional epilogue ending which follows a traditional ending and brings the essay to rest with a final anecdote or some other afterthought. The ending of E. M. Forster's "My Wood" is a conventional summary ending:

> Enormously stout, endlessly avaricious, pseudo-creative, insensely selfish, I shall weave upon my forehead the quadruple crown of possession until those nasty Bolshies come and take it off again and thrust me aside into the outer darkness.†

And G. K. Chesterton's "A Piece of Chalk" employs an even more traditional conclusion ending, one which clinches the point of the essay:

> And I stood there in a trance of pleasure, realizing that this Southern England is not only a grand peninsula, and a tradition and a civilisation; it is something even more admirable. It is a piece of chalk.‡

* From *Thoughts in the Wilderness.* Reprinted by permission of A. D. Peters & Co., London.

† From *Abinger Harvest.* Reprinted by permission of Harcourt, Brace & World, Inc. and Edward Arnold (Publishers) Ltd., London.

‡ From *Tremendous Trifles* by G. K. Chesterton, Copyright 1909, published by Sheed & Ward, Inc., New York. Reprinted by permission of Miss Dorothy Collins and the publishers.

But Wolcott Gibbs' "The Country of the Blind," an essay on the resistance of the cinema to rational criticism, terminates with the more exceptional epilogue ending:

> I once knew an educated and almost excessively cultivated man who really enjoyed reviewing the movies. He was, however, a special case, in that he was unfailingly amused in his wintry way by sex in what he was pleased to call its "contactual aspects," and the idea of an art form fundamentally based on the slow, relentless approach and final passionate collision of two enormous faces struck him as convulsing. He wrote about it all with a wonderful, maidenly distaste, and to the total bewilderment of the motion-picture industry, but he really had the time of his life. He was also a very valuable critic since, free from the terrible spell of Love, he saw a good deal that escaped his earnest colleagues.*

13) And *consider again the location of the thesis.* In the personal essay, you need not spell out your thesis at the essay's beginning, of course — but there probably should be a concise statement of your thesis at the climax or in the conclusion of your essay. Occasionally, you may even use an implied thesis — refraining from stating your thesis altogether but revealing it to your reader by indirection and suggestion. Virginia Woolf, in "The Death of the Moth," muses about the dying struggles of a diminutive moth on a window ledge with the world's great landscape beyond, concluding with what is, because of its understatement, an implied thesis — "O yes, he seemed to say, death is stronger than I am."

14) *Finally, concentrate on style and on the literary touches.* Both, of course, have been a part of your conception from the beginning. But now that the larger problems of form are solved, you can turn more of your rewriting time over to these. See if there is any point where an image, metaphor, symbol, quotation, allusion, play on words could be sharper or richer. Do all you can to make the wording smooth and clear, possibly even lyrical or grand. Certainly at the essay's climax you will

consider using the most impressive language that it will bear. At the same time, you will be consistent. Unless you are being inconsistent for effect, try to maintain the same general level of diction and the same general sentence and paragraph style throughout the essay. In the beginning of your essay, you commit yourself to a certain style and a certain approach throughout your essay. Do not violate this commitment without good reason. At any rate, the personal essay is a literary form — and this implies a heightened vision and language not to be achieved in any quick and easy way. Even the poetry of G. K. Chesterton's "A Piece of Chalk" is possible in the personal essay:

> With my stick and my knife, my chalks and my brown paper, I went out on to the great downs. I crawled across those colossal contours that express the best quality of England, because they are at the same time soft and strong. The smoothness of them has the same meaning as the smoothness of great cart-horses, or the smoothness of the beech-tree; it declares in the teeth of our timid and cruel theories that the mighty are merciful. As my eye swept the landscape, the landscape was as kindly as any of its cottages, but for power it was like an earthquake. The villages in the immense valley were safe, one could see, for centuries; yet the lifting of the whole land was like the lifting of one enormous wave to wash them all away.
>
> I crossed one swell of living turf after another, looking for a place to sit down and draw. Do not, for heaven's sake, imagine I was going to sketch from Nature. I was going to draw devils and seraphim, and blind old gods that men worshipped before the dawn of right, and saints in robes of angry crimson, and seas of strange green, and all the sacred or monstrous symbols that look so well in bright colours on brown paper. They are much better worth drawing than Nature; also they are much easier to draw. When a cow came slouching by in the field next to me, a mere artist might have drawn it; but I always get wrong in the hind legs of quadrupeds. So I drew the soul of the cow; which I saw there plainly walking before me in the sunlight; and the soul was

all purple and silver, and had seven horns and the mystery that belongs to all the beasts. But though I could not with a crayon get the best out of the landscape, it does not follow that the landscape was not getting the best out of me. And this, I think, is the mistake that people make about the old poets who lived before Wordsworth, and were supposed not to care very much about Nature because they did not describe it much.

They preferred writing about great men to writing about great hills; but they sat on the great hills to write it. They gave out much less about Nature, but they drank in, perhaps, much more. They painted the white robes of their holy virgins with the blinding snow, at which they had stared all day. They blazoned the shields of their paladins with the purple and gold of many heraldic sunsets. The greenness of a thousand green leaves clustered into the live green figure of Robin Hood. The blueness of a score of forgotten skies became the blue robes of the Virgin. The inspiration went in like sunbeams and came out like Apollo.*

15) *Now look again at the essay* — especially at the first sentence of your essay and the last, and at the title. The first sentence — whether it leads the reader directly into a consideration of your subject or is part of a prelude — should arouse the reader's curiosity. The last sentence should have about it a ring of finality, of farewell. And the title should be brief, descriptive or at least pertinent, and provocative. Above all, the essay should possess the kind of literary sophistication readers expect to find in the form.

If you get stuck along the way, as all writers do from time to time, here are some suggestions: 1) Go back to the beginning of the creative process and retrace your steps, checking at each point to see that you have made the best decision. Perhaps you made a wrong turn somewhere. 2) Forget about the immediate problem for the time being, loosen up and just write on — perhaps the problem will iron itself out, or perhaps you will be

* From *Tremendous Trifles* by G. K. Chesterton, Copyright 1909, published by Sheed & Ward, Inc., New York. Reprinted by permission of Miss Dorothy Collins and the publishers.

able to deal with it better later. 3) Come back to it later. Writing is hard work, perhaps you need to take a short rest from it. When you turn again to your essay, you may be able to deal more successfully with problems as they come up. 4) If you are really stuck, stop writing and start reading. See how other essayists have dealt with their materials. It may help if you use another essay as a model. 5) As last resort, put this essay aside and start afresh on a new idea.

An Exemplary Personal Essay

Once More to the Lake

E. B. White

One summer, along about 1904, my father rented a camp on a lake in Maine and took us all there for the month of August. We all got ringworm from some kittens and had to rub Pond's Extract on our arms and legs night and morning, and my father rolled over in a canoe with all his clothes on; but outside of that the vacation was a success and from then on none of us ever thought there was any place in the world like that lake in Maine. We returned summer after summer — always on August 1st for one month. I have since become a salt-water man, but sometimes in summer there are days when the restlessness of the tides and the fearful cold of the sea water and the incessant wind which blows across the afternoon and into the evening make me wish for the placidity of a lake in the woods. A few weeks ago this feeling got so strong I bought myself a couple of bass hooks and a spinner and returned to the lake where we used to go, for a week's fishing and to revisit old haunts.

I took along my son, who had never had any fresh water up his nose and who had seen lily pads only from train windows. On the journey over to the lake I began to wonder what it would be like. I wondered how time would have marred this unique, this holy spot — the coves and streams, the hills that the sun set behind, the camps and the paths behind the camps. I was sure that the tarred road would have found it out and I wondered in what other ways it would be desolated. It is strange how much you can remember about places like that once you allow your mind to return into the grooves which lead back. You remember one thing, and that suddenly reminds you of another thing. I guess I remembered clearest of all the early mornings, when the lake was cool and motionless, remembered how the bedroom smelled of the lumber it was made of and of the wet woods whose scent entered through the screen. The partitions in the camp were thin and did not extend clear to the top of the rooms, and as I was always the first up I would dress softly so as not to wake the others, and sneak out into the sweet outdoors and start out in the canoe, keeping close along the shore in the long shadows of the pines. I remembered being very careful never to rub my paddle against the gunwale for fear of disturbing the stillness of the cathedral.

The lake had never been what you would call a wild lake. There were cottages sprinkled around the shores, and it was in farming country although the shores of the lake were quite heavily wooded. Some of the cottages were owned by nearby farmers, and you would live at the shore and eat your meals at the farmhouse. That's what our family did. But although it wasn't wild, it was a fairly large and undisturbed lake and there were places in it which, to a child at least, seemed infinitely remote and primeval.

I was right about the tar: it led to within half a mile of the shore. But when I got back there, with my boy, and we settled into a camp near a farmhouse and into the kind of summertime I had known, I could tell that it was going to be pretty much the same as it had been before — I knew it, lying in bed the first morning, smelling the bedroom, and hearing the boy sneak quietly out and go off along the shore in a boat. I began to sustain the illusion that he was I, and therefore, by simple transposition, that I was my father. This sensation persisted, kept cropping up all the time we were there. It was not an entirely new feeling, but in this setting it grew much stronger. I seemed to be living a dual existence. I would be in the middle of some simple act, I would be picking up a bait box or laying down a table fork, or I would be saying something, and suddenly it would be not I but my father who was saying the words or making the gesture. It gave me a creepy sensation.

We went fishing the first morning. I felt the same damp moss covering the worms in the bait can, and saw the dragonfly alight on the tip of my rod as it hovered a few inches from the surface of the water. It was the arrival of this fly that convinced me beyond any doubt that everything was as it always had been, that the years were a mirage and there had been no years. The small waves were the same, chucking the rowboat under the chin as we fished at anchor, and the boat was the same boat, the same color green and the ribs broken in the same places, and under the floor-boards the same fresh-water leavings and débris — the dead helgramite, the wisps of moss, the rusty discarded fishhook, the dried blood from yesterday's catch. We stared silently at the tips of our rods, at the dragonflies that came and went. I lowered the tip of mine into the water, tentatively, pensively dislodging the fly, which darted two feet away, poised, darted two feet back, and came to rest again a little farther up the rod. There had been no years between the ducking of this dragonfly and the other one — the one that was part of memory. I looked at the boy, who was silently watching his fly, and it was my hands that held his rod, my eyes watching. I felt dizzy and didn't know which rod I was at the end of.

We caught two bass, hauling them in briskly as though they were mackerel, pulling them over the side of the boat in a businesslike manner without any landing net, and stunning them with a blow on the back of the head. When we got back for a swim before lunch, the lake was exactly where we had left it, the same number of inches from the dock, and there was only the merest suggestion of a breeze. This seemed an utterly enchanted sea, this lake you could leave to its own devices for a few hours and come back to, and find that it had not stirred, this constant and trustworthy body of water. In the shallows, the dark, water-soaked sticks and twigs, smooth and old, were undulating in clusters on the bottom against the clean ribbed sand, and the track of the mussel was plain. A school of minnows swam by, each minnow with its small individual shadow, doubling the attendance, so clear and sharp in the sunlight. Some of the other campers were in swimming, along the shore, one of them with a cake of soap, and the water felt thin and clear and unsubstantial. Over the years there had been this person with the cake of soap, this cultist, and here he was. There had been no years.

Up to the farmhouse to dinner through the teeming, dusty field, the road under our sneakers was only a two-track road. The middle track was missing, the one with the marks of the hooves and the splotches of dried, flaky manure. There had always been three tracks to choose from in choosing which track to walk in; now the choice was narrowed down to two. For a moment I missed terribly the middle alternative. But the way led past the tennis court, and something about the way it lay there in the sun reassured me; the tape had loosened along the backline, the alleys were green with plantains and other weeds, and the net (installed in June and removed in September) sagged in the dry noon, and the whole place steamed with midday heat and hunger and emptiness. There was a choice of pie for dessert, and one was blueberry and one was apple, and the waitresses were the same country girls, there having been no passage of time, only the illusion of it as in a dropped curtain — the waitresses were still fifteen; their hair had been washed, that was the only difference — they had been to the movies and seen the pretty girls with the clean hair.

Summertime, oh summertime, pattern of life indelible, the fade-proof lake, the woods unshatterable, the pasture with the sweetfern and the juniper forever and ever, summer without end; this was the background, and the life along the shore was the design, the cottages with their innocent and tranquil design, their tiny docks with the flagpole and the American flag floating against the white clouds in the blue sky, the little paths over the roots of the trees leading from camp to camp and the paths leading back to the outhouses and the can of lime for sprinkling, and at the souvenir counters at the store the miniature birch-bark canoes and the post cards that showed things looking a little better than they looked. This was the American family at play, escaping the city heat, wondering whether the newcomers in the camp at the head of the cove were "common" or "nice," wondering whether it was true that the people who drove up for Sunday dinner at the farmhouse were turned away because there wasn't enough chicken.

It seemed to me, as I kept remembering all this, that those times and those summers had been infinitely precious and worth saving.

There had been jollity and peace and goodness. The arriving (at the beginning of August) had been so big a business in itself, at the railway station the farm wagon drawn up, the first smell of the pine-laden air, the first glimpse of the smiling farmer, and the great importance of the trunks and your father's enormous authority in such matters, and the feel of the wagon under you for the long ten-mile haul, and at the top of the last long hill catching the first view of the lake after eleven months of not seeing this cherished body of water. The shouts and cries of the other campers when they saw you, and the trunks to be unpacked, to give up their rich burden. (Arriving was less exciting nowadays, when you sneaked up in your car and parked it under a tree near the camp and took out the bags and in five minutes it was all over, no fuss, no loud wonderful fuss about trunks.)

Peace and goodness and jollity. The only thing that was wrong now, really, was the sound of the place, an unfamiliar nervous sound of the outboard motors. This was the note that jarred, the one thing that would sometimes break the illusion and set the years moving. In those other summertimes all motors were inboard; and when they were at a little distance, the noise they made was a sedative, an ingredient of summer sleep. They were one-cylinder and two-cylinder engines, and some were make-and-break and some were jump-spark, but they all made a sleepy sound across the lake. The one-lungers throbbed and fluttered, and the twin-cylinder ones purred and purred, and that was a quiet sound too. But now the campers all had outboards. In the daytime, in the hot mornings, these motors made a petulant, irritable sound; at night, in the still evening when the afterglow lit the water, they whined about one's ears like mosquitoes. My boy loved our rented outboard, and his great desire was to achieve singlehanded mastery over it, and authority, and he soon learned the trick of choking it a little (but not too much), and the adjustment of the needle valve. Watching him I would remember the things you could do with the old one-cylinder engine with the heavy flywheel, how you could have it eating out of your hand if you got really close to it spiritually. Motor boats in those days didn't have clutches, and you would make a landing by shutting off the motor at the proper time and coasting in with a dead rudder. But there was a way of reversing them, if you learned the trick, by cutting the switch and putting it on again exactly on the final dying revolution of the flywheel, so that it would kick back against compression and begin reversing. Approaching a dock in a strong following breeze, it was difficult to slow up sufficiently by the ordinary coasting method, and if a boy felt he had complete mastery over his motor, he was tempted to keep it running beyond its time and then reverse it a few feet from the dock. It took a cool nerve, because if you threw the switch a twentieth of a second too soon you would catch the flywheel when it still had speed enough to go up past center, and the boat would leap ahead, charging bull-fashion at the dock.

We had a good week at the camp. The bass were biting well and the sun shone endlessly, day after day. We would be tired at night and lie down in the accumulated heat of the little bedrooms after the long hot day and the breeze would stir almost imperceptibly outside and the smell of the swamp drift in through the rusty screens. Sleep would come easily and in the morning the red squirrel would be on the roof, tapping out his gay routine. I kept remembering everything, lying in bed in the mornings — the small steamboat that had a long rounded stern like the lip of a Ubangi, and how quietly she ran on the moonlight sails, when the older boys played their mandolins and the girls sang and we ate doughnuts dipped in sugar, and how sweet the music was on the water in the shining night, and what it had felt like to think about girls then. After breakfast we would go up to the store and the things were in the same place — the minnows in a bottle, the plugs and spinners disarranged and pawed over by the youngsters from the boys' camp, the fig newtons and the Beeman's gum. Outside, the road was tarred and cars stood in front of the store. Inside, all was just as it had always been, except there was more Coca Cola and not so much Moxie and root beer and birch beer and sarsaparilla. We would walk out with a bottle of pop apiece and sometimes the pop would backfire up our noses and hurt. We explored the streams, quietly, where the turtles slid off the sunny logs and dug their way into the soft bottom; and we lay on the town wharf and fed worms to the tame bass. Everywhere we went I had trouble making out which was I, the one walking at my side, the one walking in my pants.

One afternoon while we were there at that lake a thunderstorm came up. It was like the revival of an old melodrama that I had seen long ago with childish awe. The second-act climax of the drama of the electrical disturbance over a lake in America had not changed in any important respect. This was the big scene, still the big scene. The whole thing was so familiar, the first feeling of oppression and heat and a general air around camp of not wanting to go very far away. In midafternoon (it was all the same) a curious darkening of the sky, and a lull in everything that had made life tick; and then the way the boats suddenly swung the other way at their moorings with the coming of a breeze out of the new quarter, and the premonitory rumble. Then the kettle drum, then the snare, then the bass drum and cymbals, then crackling light against the dark, and the gods grinning and licking their chops in the hills. Afterward the calm, the rain steadily rustling in the calm lake, the return of light and hope and spirits, and the campers running out in joy and relief to go swimming in the rain, their bright cries perpetuating the deathless joke about how they were getting simply drenched, and the children screaming with delight at the new sensation of bathing in the rain, and the joke about getting drenched linking the generations in a strong indestructible chain. And the comedian who waded in carrying an umbrella.

When the others went swimming my son said he was going in too. He pulled his dripping trunks from the line where they had hung all through the shower, and wrung them out. Languidly, and with no thought of going in, I watched him, his hard little body, skinny and bare, saw him wince slightly as he pulled up around his vitals the small, soggy, icy garment. As he buckled the swollen belt suddenly my groin felt the chill of death.

An Analysis

1) From what he confides of his experience, knowledge, and taste, what sort of person is E. B. White?
2) What is the tone of "Once More to the Lake"? Serious, light, fanciful, nostalgic, sentimental, ironic, humorous, lofty, intense, genial, lyrical, or something else or some combination of things?
3) What is the subject of "Once More to the Lake"?
4) Can you find a one-sentence expression of the essay's main point, the thesis? Does he state it more than once? Does he ever state it explicitly?

5) Is the specific thesis of "Once More to the Lake" related to a larger and more traditionally literary theme: that life is a paradox of change and permanence, novelty and repetition?
6) How would you describe the general form of the essay?
7) Is there a clear beginning, middle, and end?
8) What makes "Once More to the Lake" an essay and not a story even though it has a strong narrative element?
9) Are some parts of the essay more intense and lyrical than others? Which? And why?
10) What specific methods of paragraph development does E. B. White use?
11) What kind of sentences does he prefer?
12) What transitions and connections does he habitually employ in the essay?
13) What is the level of English in "Once More to the Lake" —formal, informal, colloquial?
14) E. B. White's style is simple and yet literary. How does he achieve this?
15) Is he characteristically either adverbial or adjectival?
16) Does he ever use alliteration, assonance, onomatopoeia, or other such devices of sound and rhythm?
17) What images, metaphors, symbols, allusions, quotations, anecdotes does E. B. White use? Do they help achieve a literary atmosphere?

Assignments

1) Write a three-paragraph essay on a traditional topic, one that would have appealed to Bacon or Addison.
2) Write an essay in the style of some well-known essayist, either using a particular essay as a model or simply appropriating the essayist's characteristic style.
3) Make a structural analysis of a published essay: underline every statement of the thesis with double lines, underline the topic sentence of each paragraph with single lines, circle each transition (connect by lines those working in

combination), count the number of words in each sentence (placing the result in brackets after each sentence) and the number of sentences in each paragraph (placing this result in brackets at the head of each paragraph) and place a check by the more apparent literary touches, quotations, allusions, figures of speech, etc. Now read the essay again noting the way in which form and content supplement one another.

4) Make a list of several different essays on the same subject, noting the influence of form on content.

5) Write an openly humorous or ironic essay.

5

The Formal Essay

Even in so informal a society as that of twentieth-century America, the formal essay is an important literary genre. Only the imperceptive and unduly practical writer would decide that "to be formal is to be phony" and would therefore ignore the art of the formal essay. The civilized and mature writer unhesitatingly includes the genre in his repertoire of prose forms; he trusts that even in a shirtsleeve society, submissive as it frequently is to riotous harangues, the formal essay still has its place, that there is need for the essay in which a thoughtful writer may consider public and social issues in a logical and reasonable way.

The Formal Essay as a Form

The formal essay is characterized primarily by its serious purpose, its public orientation, its orderliness, and its dispassionate style.

The *serious purpose* of the essayist is actually what brings the formal essay into being. The form emerges from the desire of the writer to speak lastingly and meaningfully to a serious-minded audience on a subject of some importance. An essential aspect of this serious purpose is the essayist's desire to educate, rather than to entertain; to stimulate intellectually rather than simply to delight.

Yet the serious didactic intentions of the formal essay must be distinguished from the informative intentions of the professional article. The formal essayist educates more by "pondering" than by "proving," and he is less likely to supply his reader with detailed information and scientific conclusions (as in the professional article), than he is to supply the reader with judgments and ideas designed to influence or change the reader's intellectual perspective. If the professional article presents data leading to a judgment, the formal essay presents judgments that lead to admonition. In the formal essay, fact is less important than the meaning of fact, and if analysis occurs it is not of a laboratory nature; the discussion is always less concerned with establishing the validity of evidence and more concerned with revealing the implications of conclusions and theses.

Serious in purpose, the formal essay is also *the most public of all prose forms:* it deals with matters in an overt way, in the social, political, and cultural forum; though it may be specialized or narrow in its range, it is never intimate or private. The formal essay is the form appropriate to the social, political, or cultural issue, and represents the discussion of a man, not involved in private reverie or confession, but involved in public debate or address.

To a certain extent, all prose forms are public — simply because they are written for an audience. But the words used by the formal essayist are especially geared "for all the World to hear," and the formal essayist meets his reader, not so much as personal friend or confidant or next-door neighbor but as fellow citizen or as fellow member of a well-defined social group speaking on matters, not of *tete-a-tete* interest, but of large value: life and death, the nature of institutions and movements, problems of government, economics, history, philosophy, art.

A good example of the public and serious subject common to the formal essay is seen in the opening paragraph of Joseph Wood Krutch's essay on "Creative America":

> The story of man's adventures and achievements on this planet can be told in many different ways. Today it is most often told in terms of his technological advances — which is to say in terms of his assumption of power over his physical environment. Sometimes it is assumed, even, that any other achievements are mere consequences of his success in this grand enterprise, and extremists have gone so far as to suggest that the measure of a civilization is simply the horsepower available per unit of population. Nevertheless, the story can also be told in various other ways such as, for instance, in terms of his beliefs, ideals, convictions, and standards of value. Sometimes, though less often, it has been told in terms of his creative imagination as revealed in his art.
> — Joseph Wood Krutch, "Creative America."*

Indeed, the formal essayist is the man speaking for the record, not to reveal himself privately and individually but to speak representatively for the society or public of which he is a part.

Speaking seriously and publicly, the formal essayist writes with *a great sense of order.* All writing, of course, demands organization and ordering of its contents, but the formal essay, more than all others, brooks few exceptions or variations from clear-cut and logical arrangement. Unlike the personal essay, that permits a certain amount of circuitous journeying from beginning to end, the formal essay marches straight through its ideas to its conclusion. The reason for this logical deliberateness is easy to understand. The very meaning of formality is the rational ordering of events or ideas or things. And formality would be drastically weakened and diluted if it gave way to entertaining digression or intriguing but obscure architecture. If one has something serious and important to say, can he endanger the clarity of his statements by trying to be clever, subtle, or mysterious in their presentation?

And it is for this reason that the formal essayist adopts in his writing a *dispassionate style.* Though the essay may have its emotional moments, the essay itself is not emotionally oriented and does not seek to make emotional appeals. And though it may urge and promulgate definite plans of action, it maintains a certain matter-of-factness in its discussion.

This does not mean that formal essays are necessarily dull or that the formal essayist always writes "with a long face in a brown mood." Ideally the formal essay tries to be neither "sleepy" nor "noisy." Like all good pieces of writing, it strives for as much vitality of manner and grace of style as possible — without confusing any of its clear-cut ideas or without delaying the deliberate revelation of its thinking. Using indeed all his literary skills, the formal essayist nevertheless makes his essay appear almost non-literary, so subdued and muted are all his manipulations of language. A glow and luster may emerge from his words, but his readers rarely comment upon his writing by saying "how beautiful"; they are far more likely to respond by saying "how true."

Picture if you will the man speaking to a large crowd (the public occasion) on the matter of rebuilding the town devastatingly destroyed by a recent flood (the serious subject): he is sincere and serious, yet his task is not to stampede the crowd into an inefficient mob; he must speak calmly yet meaningfully; he must stir emotions to the grand task; yet he knows his address is not an occasion for propaganda or advertising; he must speak to his audience's better self, rouse them to duty. The manner he takes, dispassionate but not dull, is the manner and style of the formal essay.

Consider Abraham Lincoln's *Gettysburg Address,* a formal essay in miniature. It is stirring and grandiose — without being intimate or emotional. It is serious, public, orderly, dispassionate — and extremely effective.

⁂

Historically, the formal essay has its origins in the philosophical and critical writings of the ancient world. The reflective tracts of Cicero, Seneca, Plutarch and the critical-philosophical writings of Plato, Aristotle, Horace, Quintilian, and Longinus established in Greece and Rome a tradition of serious prose statements — even though the form ranged from apologies to dialogues to confessions to letters. The tradition was continued after the fall of the classical world by such writers as Boethius, who made his great search for truth in his essay *De Consolatione Philosophiae,* and, later in the Renaissance, George Gascoigne, whose *Certayne Notes of Instruction concerning the making of verse or rhymes in English* (1575) is one of the first formal essays in English, and Philip Sidney, whose *Defence of Poesie* is one of England's first important critical essays.

Understandably the formal essay has had its grandest moments in those ages or on those occasions when public issues of great import presented themselves. John Milton, for instance, was one of the greatest writers of formal essays (both in English and in Latin), and in such an exemplary piece as his *Areopagitica* (1644), the formal essay achieved one of its greatest heights: to discuss the significant and vital issue of censorship and the "Liberty of Unlicensed Printing" Milton chose inevitably the most formal of prose forms.

Perhaps the greatest age the formal essay has ever had was in the nineteenth century, in that Victorian world dedicated to the proprieties of a meticulously ordered society. With the development of magazines in the nineteenth century (such as the *Edinburgh Review,* the *Quarterly,* the *London Magazine, Blackwood's Magazine, Fraser's Magazine*) the formal essay (both reflective and critical) had access to a public, and such men as Macaulay, DeQuincy, Carlyle, Arnold, Ruskin, Pater, Huxley, and Newman employed the form in their thoughtful discussions of mankind and manners, aesthetics and politics. Some famous nineteenth-century essays are Wordsworth's *Preface to the Lyrical Ballads* (1800), Coleridge's various chapters in *Biographia Literaria* (1817), Emerson's famous *Nature* (1836), *Essays* (1841), *Essays: Second Series* (1844), and Henry James' essays on the *Art of Fiction* (1884).

In modern society, the formal essay is, perhaps, more frequently employed when words are written to be read aloud on some public occasion — and if the spoken word, in all likelihood, is to be permanently recorded: the President's inaugural address and state of the union message, for instance. (One sterling example is the famous inaugural address of President John F. Kennedy.) Likewise, the formal essay is the literary form today of many sermons, scholarly lectures, and ceremonial speeches (addresses before the United Nations, the Queen of England's Christmas message or address to Parliament, Memorial Day speeches, high school and college commencement addresses).

How to Write the Formal Essay

In writing the formal essay you will proceed as with all compositions in your gathering of ideas, reading for information and data, organizing and outlining your thoughts, preparing first, second, even third drafts, and then giving a final stylistic polish to your work. Certain writing procedures are the same, whether one is writing a popular article, a personal essay, a critical review, or what have you. However, in writing the formal essay you will need to keep in mind some special compositional tasks — tasks that will direct your writing into this particular genre with its own characteristics and identity.

1) First of all, *write down your subject and thesis* — and confirm their seriousness and social significance. Theoretically any subject can be handled in a formal way, yet "my trip to Hawaii" seems a less suitable subject than "The growing schism between Soviet Russia and Communist China." And even the generally appropriate subject — something from the province of religion, history, politics, art, and the like — will usually be treated in its more theoretical, abstract aspect as opposed to its practical, utilitarian aspect. (Subjects and theses of an immediate, utilitarian nature are perhaps best handled in articles rather than in essays.)

2) Next, *establish clearly the projected audience and occasion for your essay.* And the best way to do so is by writing it down on paper. Ask yourself: for whom am I writing? And why? These are questions one should always ask when he writes — but especially so when writing the formal essay, for many times you will come to the formal essay more in consideration of occasion and audience than even in consideration of subject. Many times you will write the formal essay, not simply because you have a certain subject and thesis on hand, but be-

cause you need to deal with a certain audience in a certain way.

In determining audience and occasion keep these principles in mind: the formal essay is more appropriate to a well-educated audience than a poorly educated audience: the audience should have a serious interest in your subject and thesis; your audience should have a certain homogeneity, certain distinguishable values, beliefs, and behaviors in common. Also, your essay should speak to a general need; when we speak of occasion we mean, really, the *occasion of need* — the need to remind, to celebrate, to analyze, to redefine; in fact, occasions come into existence out of general need, and it is in recognizing the general need that makes us write appropriately and effectively for an occasion.

Try very hard to state in words *why* you are writing your formal essay: "because I am disturbed by the recent monetary policies of the government" or "because I think that 'God is dead' theology calls for a redefinition of God" or "because man's conquest of space climaxes man's technological revolution and raises the whole question of man's real goals in the universe." Your "because" statement is your occasion — now all you need to ask is whether or not the occasion is public and general.

Would you plan to write a formal essay if the occasion turned out to be "my delight with Christmas" or "my fondness for my eccentric old Uncle Ben" or "my animosity toward glass-and-steel architecture"? No. For such subjects — and occasions — try the popular article or personal essay instead.

3) After establishing your subject, your audience, and your occasion, you will need to *establish your role in the composition.* In writing the formal essay, one of the most important things you must establish is the "voice" or "persona" — for even though every composition has voice and persona, in the formal essay they are of a special kind.

As a formal essayist, you will suppress your unique personality, your extreme individuality, and assume the role of the representative social man and write in a manner that is essentially detached and impersonal. You may write as a twentieth-century American citizen, but not especially as a citizen of

Chicago, Illinois, in the grocery business, who attends the Methodist church. You will write as someone vitally concerned with your subject, but not as a propagandist, promoter, or special pleader. You may express personal judgments in the formal essay, but you will play down their personal quality and present them as often as possible as self-evident truths.

4) To establish your impersonal, public voice in the formal essay, *you will most frequently write in the third-person singular.* The pronouns "one" and "he" are most consistently used in formal expressions — "One may not agree with the present administration, but one does not riot on the streets in protest" or "A man may have no personal knowledge of God, but he may hesitate to attack the tradition of revelation."

In some essays, however, you may compromise the utter objectivity of the third person with the personality of the first, and use the social or editorial first-person plural: "Those of us who have lived through two world wars feel that we have seen enough of modern horror" or "We do not believe that the new eschatology will replace the old," or "As victims of mass media, we no longer distinguish very clearly between truth and falsehood."

Only rarely will you ever use the first-person singular in the formal essay. You will do so only if it is vitally necessary to present your subject and thesis *from your special perspective:* Let us say you are a prominent authority in a certain science or art and you are writing from the perspective of that special, even unique knowledge; you may indeed be forced to say "I have never found evidence that these issues are simple" or "I have come at last to the conclusion that his ideas are pernicious." But in every instance, you would be using the pronoun "I" only to the extent that you hold some public or social role appropriate to the formal essay. "I, the mayor of the city . . .," "I, the president of the student body, . . ." or "I, the minister to this congregation, . . ." If you refer to yourself in the formal essay, be sure that you hold some sort of status as far as your subject, audience, and occasion are concerned.

Robert Maynard Hutchins, speaking as a former chancellor of the University of Chicago and as President of the Fund for the Republic, U.S.A., legitimately used the first person in his essay on "Freedom and the Responsibility of the Press," originally delivered as an address:

> In 1930, some twenty-five years ago, I last had the honor of confronting the American Society of Newspaper Editors. The quarter of a century between has been the longest in history. That was a different world, before the Depression, before the New Deal, before the Newspaper Guild, before the suburbs, before they charged for newsprint, before the atom, before television. It was a world in which the press was powerful and numerous. Though the press is powerful still, some eight hundred papers that were alive then are gone. Twenty-five years hence, when I am eighty-one, where will the press be?
> — Robert Maynard Hutchins, "Freedom and the Responsibility of the Press."*

5) Once you have determined your subject, audience, occasion, and voice, you will *begin the actual composition of the essay* — assuming that you have your ideas well organized and ordered. Ideally, you will have written down on three-by-five or five-by-seven cards the individual ideas, thoughts, data, facts, judgments that you have developed in your pre-writing preparations, and you will have arranged these cards — literally and physically — into well-ordered groups that now you can simply transcribe, with the necessary elaborations and transitions, onto the manuscript page.

6) As you move from notes to the actual text of your composition, you will work within the structure of the formal essay. This structure will be essentially conservative.

First, you will write what may be termed a slow or *unhurried beginning*, taking time frequently for a certain amount of intellectual preparation before you officially announce your thesis. Your delayed beginning will not, however, be in any way oblique — for from the very first word of the formal essay you

* From *Freedom, Education, and the Fund* by Robert Maynard Hutchins, published by the World Publishing Company. Copyright © 1956 by Robert M. Hutchins. Reprinted by permission.

are committed toward a straight and direct path of exposition and discussion. In your opening words, you will declare the area of the essay's concern — the general subject matter — but you may feel that you need to make a few preliminary statements, not to entertain but to inform, to establish a context of significance, before you begin the step-by-step presentation of your thinking. While the professional article makes much greater use of direct beginnings — *here it is, this is what I'm talking about* — the formal essay, by its very meditative nature, may (without, of course, completely ruling out the direct beginning) take a slightly longer time to get completely underway.

In the following example, for instance, you will note the setting of an intellectual and philosophical stage, broad in scope, before the essay narrows to its specific discussion:

> We live in an unusual world, marked by very great and irreversible changes that occur within the span of a man's life. We live in a time where our knowledge and understanding of the world of nature grows wider and deeper at an unparalleled rate; and where the problems of applying this knowledge to man's needs and hopes are new, and only a little illuminated by our past history.
>
> Indeed it has always, in traditional societies, been the great function of culture to keep things rather stable, quiet, and unchanging. It has been the function of tradition to assimilate one epoch to another, one episode to another, even one year to another. It has been the function of culture to bring out meaning, by pointing to the constant or recurrent traits of human life, which in easier days one talked about as the eternal verities.
>
> In the most primitive societies, if one believes the anthropologists, the principal function of ritual, religion, of culture is, in fact, almost to stop change. It is to provide for the social organism which life provides in such a magic way for living organisms, a kind of homeostasis, an ability to remain intact, to respond only very little to the obvious convulsions and alternations in the world around.
>
> Today, culture and tradition have assumed a very different

intellectual and social purpose. The principal function of the most vital and living traditions today is precisely to provide the instruments of rapid change. . . . — J. Robert Oppenheimer, "On Science and Culture."*

And in this beginning, though it is much shorter, there is still a certain amount of "leading into" the essay proper:

H. G. Wells is quoted as having said, "There is no more evil thing than race prejudice. It holds more baseness and cruelty than any other error in the world." Race prejudice is bad, in the first place, because *all* prejudice is bad. Prejudice, by definition, is pre-judgment — the forming of opinion in advance of the evidence, and without knowledge of the facts: an unintelligent and unjustifiable procedure. It is bad, in the second place, because it is a manifestation of one of the worst confusions and abuses that have plagued men for generations — the misunderstanding and vicious application of the notion of race itself.

So noisesome has this jungle become that some writers seek to escape it by discarding the concept of race entirely. But this is sheer evasion; the only constructive solution lies in discovering the truth about race and facing it squarely and courageously.

In the first place. . . . — Henry Pratt Fairchild, "The Truth about Race."†

7) Likewise, your *conclusion* will not be abrupt, but will neatly tie the essay together, either summarizing or evaluating or coming to logical conclusion. Sometimes the ending is slightly longer than the ending of a personal essay or popular article — simply because in the formal essay all structural parts (beginning, middle, conclusion) are more definitely and clearly marked and maintained. You may, in the formal essay, take your time to conclude.

* From *Encounter*, October, 1962. Reprinted by permission of *Encounter*.

† Copyright © 1944, by Harper's Magazine, Inc. Reprinted from the October, 1944 issue of *Harper's Magazine*.

Here is a standard conclusion to a formal essay — an essay that discusses the subject of "Morals, religion, and higher education," for some 7000 words and then comes to these final paragraphs:

> How, then, can higher education escape dogmatism, narrowness, the invasion of academic freedom, and failure in its proper intellectual task and still do its duty by morals and religion? A possible answer lies in the Great Conversation. The Great Conversation began with the Greeks, the Hebrews, the Hindus, and the Chinese and has continued to the present day. It is a conversation that deals, perhaps more extensively than it deals with anything else, with morals and religion. The questions of the nature and existence of God, the nature and destiny of man, and the organization and purpose of human society are the recurring themes of the Great Conversation.
>
> There may be many ways in which a college or university can continue the Great Conversation, but it would seem offhand that one of the best ways is through the reading and discussion by all the students of the books in which the Great Conversation has been carried on by the greatest men who have taken part in it. I emphasize discussion because of the contributions that this method makes to the moral and intellectual habits we desire; and I emphasize reading and discussion by all the students and faculty because in this way the formation of a community can be advanced. To continue and enrich the Great Conversation is the object of higher education.
>
> The Civilization of the Dialogue is the only civilization worth having and the only civilization in which the whole world can unite. It is, therefore, the only civilization we can hope for, because the world must unite or be blown to bits. The Civilization of the Dialogue requires communication. It requires a common language and a common stock of ideas. It assumes that every man has reason and that every man can use it. It preserves to every man his independent judgment and, since it does so, it deprives any man or any group of men of the privilege of forcing their judgment upon any other

man or group of men. The Civilization of the Dialogue is the negation of force. We have reached the point, in any event, when force cannot unite the world; it can merely destroy it. Through continuing and enriching the Great Conversation higher education not only does its duty by morals and religion; it not only performs its proper intellectual task: it also supports and symbolizes the highest hopes and the highest aspirations of mankind. — Robert Maynard Hutchins, "Morals, Religion, and Higher Education."*

8) As for the *middle* or fundamental section of your essay, you will *match structure to content:* what you have to say will determine the design and organization of your materials.

If for instance you are writing on "The Consequences of American Involvement in Asian Affairs," the structure of your essay may rather inevitably proceed through an identification of the various consequences, and since the consequences are, in all likelihood, going to be of differing value and significance, you will probably proceed in some sort of climactic order. The structure of the middle section of your essay may well look something like this:

Discussion of First Consequence (150 words)
Discussion of Second Consequence (275 words)
Discussion of Third Consequence (300 words)
Discussion of Fourth Consequence (325 words)
Discussion of Fifth Consequence (450 words)

Or if you are writing an address to be delivered on the occasion of a Beethoven birthday celebration the structure of your essay may follow directly from your thesis, say: "Beethoven remains a 'modern composer' because the diversity of his achievements permits him to speak to generation after generation in one way or another." Inevitably the structure of your essay will be built upon the "diversity of his achievements" and you may come up with the following outline for your writing:

* From *Freedom, Education, and the Fund* by Robert Maynard Hutchins, published by the World Publishing Company. Copyright © 1956 by Robert M. Hutchins. Reprinted by permission.

Part I: Beethoven's achievement as a performer and creative artist.
- Beethoven's achievement as a conductor (150 words)
- Beethoven's achievement as a pianist (250 words)
- Beethoven's achievement as a composer (425 words)

Part II: Beethoven's achievement in musical forms.
- Beethoven's achievement in opera (100 words)
- Beethoven's achievement in chamber music (250 words)
- Beethoven's achievement in concerti (375 words)
- Beethoven's achievement in the symphony (550 words)

Part III: Beethoven's achievement in instrumentation.
- Beethoven's achievement in writing for tympani and brass (175 words)
- Beethoven's achievement in writing for the human voice (200 words)
- Beethoven's achievement in writing for string instruments (300 words)
- Beethoven's achievement in writing for piano (400 words)
- Beethoven's achievement in writing for full orchestra (650 words)

The over-all essay might finally look like this:

Beginning — The occasion for the address; statement of subject and thesis.

Middle — Part I: Beethoven as Performer — 825 words
- Part II: Beethoven's Musical Forms — 1275 words
- Part III: Beethoven's Instruments — 2725 words

Conclusion — Summary of Middle Section, and Restatement of Thesis.

In addition to this topical arrangement, however, you may note that traditionally the formal essay, once past the beginning, establishes the basic situation or problem upon which the essay is based; that is, establishes the seriousness, the sense of occasion, that the audience needs to understand in order to understand your discussion. Then follows a detailed demonstration or proving of the situation, problem, issue in question. And finally, before the conclusion, comes the evaluation, judgment, analysis, criticism of the matter. This traditional arrangement of the formal essay is, of course, the arrangement found in classical rhetoric — where the parts are called the exordium, narration, confirmation, refutation, and conclusion.*

9) With your structure established (topical or traditional) you will — as in all writing — need to *expand your basic ideas* into the full body of your composition. But in the formal essay you will be less inclined to expand your ideas by horizontal movement; you will rely more heavily on vertical exploration. That is to say, you will be less inclined to "go on to the next possible idea" and will concentrate rather on in-depth exploration of any given thought. Whereas in the popular article there may be a kind of rushing from one idea to another, an exciting dash toward conclusion, in the formal essay there is a slower movement, a more deliberate examination of illustrative and explanatory material, a greater desire to make sure that no misunderstanding occurs about the ideas that you present. Whereas in other prose forms the quantity of facts and data may be extremely valuable, in the formal essay quantity gives way to quality.

10) After you have developed your essay into something like its final shape, *you want to pay careful attention to your transitions.* Moving from paragraph to paragraph, from idea to idea, you will want to use transitions that are very clear — you should leave no doubt in your reader's mind how you are getting from one idea to another. Yet your transitions should not be hard and monotonous: though your essay will be so well-

* For a clear and detailed discussion of this traditional structure you may wish to read Professor Edward P. J. Corbett's useful book *Classical Rhetoric for the Modern Student,* New York: Oxford University Press, 1965.

organized you may easily use such indications of transitions as "one," "two," "three" or "first," "second," and "third," such words have the connotation of the scholarly or technical article and are usually to be avoided, or at least supplemented or varied, in the more formal composition. Use "one," "two," "first," "second," if you wish, in certain areas of your essay, but also manage to use prepositional phrases and conjunctive adverbs and subordinate clauses and brief transitional paragraphs to achieve your momentum and continuity. Clarity and variety together are what you want.

11) And finally in your writing of the formal essay you will take care with your rhetorical profile — that is, with the entire complex of tone and style that comes out of your vocabulary and your sentence and paragraph structures.*

Consider your words, for instance. Formal essays are generally written on the formal level of language, with a precise and thorough manner of expression. And you will use a rich, full-range of vocabulary — monosyllabic and polysyllabic words, words of Greek, Latin, and Anglo-Saxon origin, common and unusual words. But if your vocabulary leans in any direction, let it lean toward the learned and the allusive, and avoid (save for very special effects) contractions, colloquialisms, slang, or jargon. You would probably not use these words — "We don't think too many jet-set darlings are going to contribute to a true 'peace on earth' " — but rather these — "We believe that very few of today's affluent and uncommitted young men and women, devoted as they are to pleasure and play, will make any sort of serious contribution to a lasting 'peace on earth.' " Not that the first version is wrong, but it would be inappropriate in a formal essay; its words are too heavy with connotation, they are too emotive. Likewise avoid words too specialized, technical, or childish.

A typical example of formal vocabulary is found in this passage from the work of Carl Becker:

> The natural rights philosophy made its way in America with far less opposition than it did in Europe. It was accepted as

* For an extended discussion of rhetorical profile you may wish to see Weathers and Winchester, *The Strategy of Style*, New York: McGraw-Hill, 1967.

> a convenient theory for justifying the political separation of the American colonies from Great Britain; but with that object attained no further revolution of serious import, such as occurred in France, was required to bring the social and political institutions of the United States into harmony with the philosophy that presided at its birth as an independent nation. The state and Federal constitutions were scarcely more than a codification of colonial institutions with the Parliament and king left out, and the natural rights philosophy of the Declaration of Independence was accepted without much opposition as the obvious and necessary foundation of the new political structure. If the colonies had ever been governed by a king, it was only by a king *in absentia* exercising a merely nominal control. Monarchical absolutism and the theory of divine right, the vested interest of a ruling landed aristocracy based on birth, the moral and political influence of an organized state religion — none of these obstacles to political and social democracy, which had to be overcome in all European countries, was ever in any real sense a part of the American political practice or tradition. — Carl Becker, *The American Political Tradition**

12) *Consider now the structure of your sentences.* You are free, even in formal style, to write any kind of sentence you wish — elliptical, loose, simple, long, short. But note that your sentences should *not be predominantly* short, simple, elliptical: you should be sure that enough long, complex, and periodic sentences occur to handle the seriousness of your subject matter. Also, sentences in the formal essay are generally more studied and structured: you will find in formal style more of the definitely recognizable rhetorical devices of balance, parallelism, antithesis, anaphora, rhetorical question, and the like. Some examples of formally structured sentences are these:

> In the Renaissance, art is so available and so evident that those productive years of the fifteenth, sixteenth, and seventeenth centuries in Italy, France, and England offer us advantageous examples in a discussion of what art is and what the creation of it involves.

> Art is the making intellectually — even emotionally — bearable that which is otherwise not bearable, to wit — the black and the white, the agony and the joy, the birth and the death.
>
> Some poetry is prose, some prose is poetry.
>
> After the literature of the absurd, what shall we have? After the literature of sadism, what shall we be given? The future of American letters remains in question.
>
> Critics themselves need critics. Never should the judgments of the few go unchallenged by the many.

13) Likewise your *paragraphs are going to be relatively longer* than paragraphs in the popular article or the informal essay, and your paragraphs will be more definitely structured, more decisively controlled in their expansion; you will more rigidly adhere to the traditional construction of the paragraph — topic sentence and examples, topic sentence and illustrations, topic sentence and relevant details.

A representative formal paragraph is the following from Thomas Babington Macaulay — representative both in its conventional structure and in its length.

> The Puritans were men whose minds had derived a peculiar character from the daily contemplation of superior beings and eternal interests. Not content with acknowledging, in general terms, an overruling Providence, they habitually ascribed every event to the will of the Great Being, for whose power nothing was too vast, for whose inspection nothing was too minute. To know him, to serve him, to enjoy him, was with them the great end of existence. They rejected with contempt the ceremonious homage which other sects substituted for the pure worship of the soul. Instead of catching occasional glimpses of the Deity through an obscuring veil, they aspired to gaze full on his intolerable brightness, and to commune with him face to face. Hence originated their contempt for terrestrial distinctions. The difference between the greatest and the meanest of mankind seemed to vanish, when compared with the boundless interval which separated the whole race from him on whom their own eyes were constantly fixed.

They recognized no title to superiority but his favour; and confident of that favour, they despised all the accomplishments and all the dignities of the world. If they were unacquainted with the works of philosophers and poets, they were deeply read in the oracles of God. If their names were not found in the registers of heralds, they were recorded in the Book of Life. If their steps were not accompanied by a splendid train of menials, legions of ministering angels had charge over them. Their palaces were houses not made with hands; their diadems crowns of glory which should never fade away. On the rich and the eloquent, on nobles and priests, they looked down with contempt: for they esteemed themselves rich in a more precious treasure, and eloquent in a more sublime language, nobles by the right of an earlier creation, and priests by the imposition of a mightier hand. The very meanest of them was a being to whose fate a mysterious and terrible importance belonged, on whose slightest action the spirits of light and darkness looked with anxious interest, who had been destined, before heaven and earth were created, to enjoy a felicity which should continue when heaven and earth should have passed away. Events which short-sighted politicians ascribed to earthly causes had been ordained on his account. For his sake empires had risen, and flourished, and decayed. For his sake the Almighty had proclaimed his will by the pen of the Evangelist, and the harp of the prophet. He had been wrested by no common deliverer from the grasp of no common foe. He had been ransomed by the sweat of no vulgar agony, by the blood of no earthly sacrifice. It was for him that the sun had been darkened, that the rocks had been rent, that the dead had risen, that all nature had shuddered at the sufferings of her expiring God.
— Thomas Babington Macaulay, *The History of England*.

14) And one concluding word about *length in general:* because formal essays have a tendency to be more full-bodied, more complete than other prose forms — and therefore longer; because formal essays, avoiding in their seriousness the superficial and slight, give full expression to ideas and concepts — and are therefore longer; because of this frequent length of the

form, you do not want to make the mistake of padding out your material to make it look bulky and substantial and pseudo-formal. In your attempt to be formal and serious and orderly and public, you may over-write, put on unnecessary airs, and effect pomposity rather than profundity.

Your final task then, in writing the formal essay, is to go over your last draft carefully — prune and trim your words, remove mere verbiage, and tighten up your style. One should always do this in writing, of course — but the temptation *not* to do it seems especially great with this genre. Make sure your formal essay has no idle word — but is as perfectly and meaningfully wrought as possible.

An Exemplary Formal Essay

The Sorry State of History

J. H. Plumb

Quips from Cicero are uncommon in the engineers' lab; Ahab and Jael rarely provide a parable for biologists; and few civil servants seek a guide for policy in the examples of Jefferson or Pitt. Yet a hundred, or even fifty, years ago a tradition of culture, based on the classics, on Scripture, on history and literature, bound the educated classes together and projected the image of a gentleman.

It was a curious mixture of humanistic principles and national pride. The Renaissance made literary breeding fashionable; a gentleman was expected to be conversant with all knowledge, well-read in Plato and Cicero, from whom he obtained his sense of civic virtues, familiar with the Scriptures as a never-ending source of

From *Horizon Magazine*, September, 1963. Reprinted by permission of the author.

parable and aphorism, fortified in his patriotism by the story of his nation's heroes, his experience deepened and enriched by his extensive knowledge of his country's literature.

These subjects — History, Classics, Literature, and Divinity — were, with Mathematics, the core of the educational system and believed to have peculiar virtues in providing politicians, civil servants, administrators, and legislators. In them, in England certainly, the arcane wisdom of the Establishment was preserved and handed down from generation to generation.

Alas, the rising tide of scientific and industrial societies, combined with the battering of two world wars, has shattered the confidence of humanists in their capacity to lead or to instruct. Uncertain of their social function, their practitioners have taken refuge in two desperate courses — both suicidal. Either they blindly cling to their traditional attitudes and pretend that their function is what it was and that all will be well so long as change is repelled, or they retreat into their private professional world and deny any social function to their subject.

And so the humanities are at the crossroads, at a crisis in their existence; either they must change the image that they present, adapt themselves to the needs of a society dominated by science and technology, or retreat into social triviality. This is the crucial problem facing all the subjects — History, Classics, Literature — that are to be discussed here.

Adaptation is the great difficulty. Homer sells millions; Thucydides hundreds of thousands; even Tacitus tens of thousands. The hunger to know about the ancient world is almost insatiable. The professional classicists, however, rarely provide the diet (more often than not the providers live on the fringe of the profession). The professionals prefer to cherish their ancient skills, to concentrate their abilities on turning a piece of Burke into Ciceronian prose or on similar masterpieces of obvious triviality.

As with classics, so with history: the demand to know about the past is greater than ever before in human history, but it is rarely the professionals who satisfy it. It is more often gifted amateurs such as Mrs. Woodham-Smith or Christopher Herold. In spite of the acerbities of Dr. F. R. Leavis, Sir Charles Snow's opponent, tens of thousands still enjoy Galsworthy, Wells, or Bennett; ordinary men and women still search for their imaginative satisfactions in the whole of the world's literature, untouched by the corrosive acid of literary criticism.

Yet perhaps the situation is worst of all in my own subject — History. For this reason: it has lost all faith in itself as a guide to the actions of men; no longer do historians investigate the past in the hope that it may enable their fellow men to control the future. Its educational value, they feel, lies in the exercises it provides for the mind and not in what it contains. History, well taught, they argue, is admirable discipline in clear and precise thinking. It extends the memory, sharpens the sense of logic, teaches the rules of evidence, and gives practice in lucid exposition and clarity of thought.

And these exercises, they maintain, can best be performed on subjects upon which historians have been active the longest or where the source material — as in medieval history — makes the greatest demands on these faculties. Therefore, it is the old, tried subjects — English history, European, medieval, and modern — that must provide the core of historical education.

Within this core, it seems, there are certain problems which, because scholarly talent has battened on them for decades, make the best exercises of all for historical training; hence the importance of certain topics that bewilder most outsiders and often reduce others to uncomprehending mirth, such as endless discussions of the importance of the coronation of Charlemagne on Christmas Day, 800, or whether or not the accession of George III brought about a break in constitutional practice.

So sixth-form English schoolboys will be familiar with the entire historiography of the controversies about George III from Horace Walpole to Sir Lewis Namier, yet remain totally ignorant of the scientific revolution of the seventeenth century, or even — and this, too, is quite possible — of the Industrial and American revolutions in George III's own reign. To the American counterparts of these sixth-formers, of course, George III will remain, apparently, perpetually the villain, and nothing more, in that last revolution.

Of course, the educative argument is spurious: memory, sense of logic, critical use of evidence, lucidity in exposition — all can be trained by large subjects as well as small, by problems relevant to modern society as well as by matters indifferent. But the whole sickening, deadening process of increasing specialization within history destroys half its value for education in its broadest and best sense; the major purpose of historical studies should not be to produce professional historians, but to explain the past for our time and generation and by so doing deepen human experience and breed confidence in the capacity of man to master his environment.

And if it is to do this, what it teaches must be central, not peripheral, to the human story and concerned with the whole history of mankind and not with patriotic enclaves. Then and then only will the study of history be meaningful to the scientists, social as well as natural, who are going to dominate our society.

Although a reorganization of what is taught in the schools and in the universities might diminish the present crisis in historical studies and help to bridge the chasm between professional history and public needs, it would not solve the problem. The root of the trouble lies deeper.

One of the greatest recent successes on Broadway is Edward Albee's *Who's Afraid of Virginia Woolf?*, an appealing title for a savage, grim, searing, three-hour dialogue between a historian and his wife. The personal situation, dominated by a screeching Earth Mother (the historian's wife), provides the focus of the play's power, but its magnetism, the disquiet it breeds, derives from its deeper implications.

The historian of the play is sterile and impotent. He talks endlessly of an imagined child (the Future) and babbles bewilderingly about his past. Did he or did he not kill his parents? There is a conflict of evidence, and great uncertainty. No one, including himself, can ever know. His wife, who possesses all the force, the violence, the passion, of an instinctively living woman, hates his failure, his verbosity, his inadequacy. But her desire is also strong, and she cannot disentangle herself from his needs.

History and Life, therefore, are doomed to live it out in hate, in distrust, in mutual failure. They are lost in timeless falsehood, bound by dreams of the past that may not have existed, and enslaved by their own lies about the future. And this, as the audience streams out into the flashing neon lights of Broadway, seems to have the force of truth. History is without meaning, without power, without hope. The present exists: the past is our own cloud-cuckoo-land. Albee presents dramatically what most historians and philosophers of history believe. That is the cruel truth. He merely puts symbolically and more harshly what R. G. Collingwood and Benedetto Croce preached elsewhere.

Toward the end of the nineteenth century historians both in Europe and in America began to reject the idea that history possessed any meaning, any purpose, any dialectical pattern. Just as the novelists withdrew their interest from man in society to investigate the stream of consciousness, and painters rejected the traditions of European art for a more personal exploration of reality, so the historians came to accept that history, all history, was but a personal vision, that the past could not exist separate from themselves; what existed was a personal reconstruction of the past; all history, to quote Croce, the great Italian historian and philosopher, was present history, a contemporary construction, and so a world entire unto itself, true only for one time and one place.

As might be expected, there has been a minority of historians, largely those who concern themselves with economic history, who have resisted this attitude and maintained that the study of history could mean more than a personal world. But they have tended to argue that function and not dialectic was the true goal of history; i.e., that historians should be more concerned with the interrelations of society at a given epoch and not with those aspects which might, or might not, lead it to develop into something different.

Such an attitude is inimical to the concept of progress, or of history having much social value; so, too, is the other fashionable view which has shown great resilience in this century: the belief that history can only be explained as the working of Providence. But, as man cannot understand the mind of God or know His purpose, we must accept history as it is and regard historical analysis as little better than a guttering candle in a fathomless cave. Only at the Day of Judgment will light blaze forth. Therefore, to try to impose a pattern on history, to attempt to extract useful, broad generalizations for the guidance of man, is understandably human but intellectual folly. These, with a plethora of variations, are by and large the basic attitudes of the profession. And most of them are not very far from Albee's.

Even if the professionals hold up their hands in horror at the idea of drawing lessons from history, others, far less capable, do not. Toynbee has no hesitation in trampling where Namier feared to tread. And before Toynbee, Spengler displayed no less confidence and no less absurdity. Both regarded history as a whirligig in which decay was as frequent as growth.

Toynbee dismisses the last four hundred years of European history as an uninterrupted disaster; Spengler declared in 1928 that the West was in its "sunset epoch," that the world had gone straight downhill since the eighteenth century. Both of them encouraged despair about the present, neither considered material progress as relevant. They were Albee's progenitors, if anyone; and their vision of history persists, and distorts the truth.

Yet if there is one idea that makes sense of history, it is the idea of progress. The idea is simple: over the centuries, in spite of frequent setbacks, the material condition of man has improved. Men live longer, get more to eat, are freer from disease, possess more leisure. The speed of progress has accelerated phenomenally over the past one hundred fifty years and shows all prospect of continuing to do so. Place a hand loom by a computer; the case is unarguable.

With this material progress has gone an increase in civility. And this, many, for obvious reasons, find difficult to believe. To those not well grounded in history but conscious of Hitler's Jewish policy, two world wars, and Hiroshima — to say nothing of Guernica, Lidice, Stalin's camps, the Warsaw Ghetto, and the continuing bestialities of men — this claim may appear almost naïvely optimistic. Yet it is true. The world is less savage, less brutal, less tyrannical than it was a hundred years ago.

How progress has happened and is happening is complex, not entirely understood, but it is certainly the most intellectually fascinating aspect of history. It ought to be the core of historical study and education, particularly the latter. It relates directly to the scientific and technical world in which we live. And furthermore the interpretation of how this has happened and might be accelerated would give a renewed sense of social purpose to the teaching of history. The history of progress, well taught, would at least breed confidence in the present and the future, dispel Albee's nightmare, and fortify those qualities in man that have helped him to drag himself from the cave to the industrial suburb. But there lies the rub.

To many the idea that men should pursue material progress is an anathema: for them, as for Toynbee, it is vulgar; destructive of spiritual values; repellent in its social and artistic manifestations; totally destructive of what the good Dr. Leavis calls the "organic community."

Now the opposition to the idea of progress, conscious or unconscious, derives from three of its aspects. It is essentially secular; it is socially radical; it is, wrongly, assumed to be tainted with Marxism. (Its father, however, was not Marx but Francis Bacon, an almost respectable capitalist.)

Certainly progress has quickened when man has applied his deductive powers to the material world, whether it has been to the method of working flints or to making electricity. The more scientific his approach to the problems of his environment, the more speedily has he solved them. Neither prayer nor exorcism will stop smallpox, but vaccination will.

The idea of progress is essentially materialist and makes an uneasy bedfellow for religion: wisely, Pius IX anathematized the idea in 1864.

However, the social radicalism implied in the idea of progress has probably been a greater enemy than its rationalism. And this is particularly true of this century. Industrialization impels social change: old certainties of class, status, education, get washed away. Nor is it a gentle process: it has in its early stages been as brutal as any historical movement. Slums, industrial tyranny, a ravaged countryside, speak too vividly of its evils. Sensitive men, bred in middle-class traditions, frightened for their values and their status, have lost all sense of historical judgment. They have fled to a never-never land of rustic glory where every peasant is a craftsman and — no matter how illiterate — radiates with "inner life." Or, like the New England historians of the nineteenth century, they have escaped into a bogus medievalism that exalts Mont-Saint-Michel as the pinnacle of human achievement.

Yet such absurd attitudes, understandable as they are, and propagated endlessly by Dr. Leavis and his disciples, are eagerly believed. They are taught day in, day out, in our schools and universities, and swallowed wholesale. Do such men know nothing of the past or of the sheer horror of pre-industrial society: its filth, its disease, its hunger, the brutishness of its pleasures, its frustrations, its tyrannies, its gross superstitions? Do they never look at Bruegel or Hogarth or even Rowlandson? Do they never read?

Would it surprise them to learn that, in the societies they adulate, dying Negroes were thrown by the score into the Atlantic for the sake of the insurance; that small girls and boys were strung up on gibbets for petty theft; that men were castrated, disembowelled, and quartered in public; that these were not exceptional events but commonplace and repeated without protest?

Such happenings might be matched by incidents of evil and cruelty today, but these rarely pass unrecorded and rightly create a sense of public horror. They are not accepted as a part of life, like the seasons, unchanging and unchangeable, as they were in the pre-industrial societies of Europe and America. (Indeed, to think that a peasant's life was more enriching than a modern factory-worker's borders on lunacy.) Yet hardly a historian's voice has been raised at this constant denigration of the present or at the corruption of scholarship that passes as literary and social criticism.

This would not matter if it were a minor eccentricity of a few literary critics or reactionary historians, but it is only the most aggressive aspect of a general attitude. Most current teaching in the humanities undermines confidence not only in present society — that is of no great importance — but in those qualities by which man has bettered himself: technical cunning, applied intelligence, and a capacity to risk change.

Instruction of this kind makes scientists impatient of the humanities and leads them to dismiss them as absurd or trivial or both. There is a growing danger, as science grows, of their being pushed farther into the academic background. Yet if ever there was need for the humanities, it is now, before the educational system required by a scientific society sets in a rigid pattern.

To many influential sections of Western society, particularly Western European society, industrialism and its concomitants are distasteful, not merely in their manifestations — no one would pretend that industry does not bring plenty of horrors in its wake — but in their essence. They wish to reject them. They prefer to retain the social and cultural exclusiveness of an agrarian and commercial society, of the world of Jane Austen, of Anthony Trollope, of Thomas Arnold and Rudyard Kipling. Hence the cult of D. H. Lawrence, who was but a gifted beatnik version of Thoreau or W. H. Hudson, men who loved life and hated humanity, men of sensitive hearts and thick heads.

Although this crisis in the humanities primarily springs from the nature of our backward-looking, tradition-drugged society, it has been encouraged by the treason of historians to their subject. They have permitted, almost without protest, a false image of history to be projected. Except as mind-trainers they have almost contracted out of education, leaving to others, and to others far less worthy, the formulation of a social attitude to the world about us.

It is an odd situation. Technically, history has never been so superbly equipped. Its methods are more refined, its practitioners more skilled, its knowledge greater and more exact than ever before in the long record of man. Yet rarely has history been so socially impotent.

And some responsibility must lie on its own shoulders, on the reticence of historians, their ambiguities, their reluctance to accept the social responsibilities that their subject imposes on them, and their adamantine conservatism toward the teaching of history.

Yet as humanity crawls up the face of the Eiger, hesitates, slips, and then miraculously scrambles back, it seems a little hard that those who plot its course should give no encouragement.

An Analysis

1) What is the "occasion" for this essay?
2) Where in the essay does Plumb first announce his subject?
3) To what sort of audience does Plumb assume he is talking? Cite evidence to support your conclusion.
4) What is the "thesis" of this essay?
5) When does the first clear statement of the "problem" to be discussed occur?
6) Is this essay a serious piece of writing? How can you tell? How *soon* can you tell?
7) What significance do the references to Cicero, Ahab, Jael and so forth have in the first paragraph of this essay in establishing the work as a formal essay?
8) In addition to the capitalized allusions themselves, what other words in the first paragraph are especially appropriate to the formal essay?

9) In what way is this essay "public"? To what extent do the words "civil servants," "educated classes," "tradition," "culture," "national pride," "patriotism," and the like in the first few paragraphs establish a "public" tone?

10) In the eighth paragraph, Plumb uses the first-person singular pronoun. What justification is there for this use? Does the use of "my" spoil the objectivity of the formal essay?

11) How many paragraphs constitute the Beginning of this essay?

12) How many paragraphs constitute the Ending of this essay?

13) What sort of conclusion does the essay have? Does it summarize what has already been said? Does it evaluate what has been said? Does it come to some logical or rational conclusion? Does it introduce some new idea?

14) Count the number of words in each sentence in three random paragraphs in the essay. What is the average number of words in each sentence?

15) Can you make any observations about the structure of the sentences? Are they generally loose or generally periodic? Are they generally simple, compound, complex?

16) The formal essay makes use of many rhetorical constructions and devices. In paragraphs thirty-one and thirty-two, what particular — and obvious — rhetorical device is being used? How effective is this use?

17) Locate some other easily recognized rhetorical and stylistic devices — such as balance, parallelism, antithesis.

18) Analyze all the rhetorical and stylistic implications of the following sentence from the essay: "Toynbee has no hesitation in trampling where Namier feared to tread."

19) Note the careful use of transition words in this essay. How many paragraphs, for instance, begin with such words or phrases as "of course," "however," "yet," "then"?

20) Examine carefully the vocabulary of this essay. What is its range? Can you find any slang words? Contractions? Highly technical words?

21) How does this essay differ from a professional article? Consider the kind of evidence and information employed in the discussion. Consider also the use of details.

22) Comment on the absence of notes and bibliography in this essay. Do you think Plumb should have told the reader exactly where all his data and information are to be found?

Assignments

1) Make a list of twelve to fifteen subjects that would be suitable for discussion in a formal essay. Indicate for each subject, the sense of need or occasion that lifts it to the formal level.

2) Looking through the last twelve issues of such magazines as *The American Scholar, Yale Review, Horizon,* or *The Centennial Review,* locate at least three formal essays and determine as precisely as possible what each essay is trying to do: criticize, celebrate, inspire, reform.

3) Choose a formal essay that especially appeals to you and make an analysis of its structure; that is, identify beginning, middle, and end — as well as subject and thesis. How well organized is the essay? How easy is it to outline?

4) Choose a formal essay that especially appeals to you and make an analysis of its language. Select three paragraphs, one from the beginning, one from the middle, and one from the end. By listing, counting, and comparing, describe as best you can the vocabulary, the sentences, and the paragraphs used in the essay.

5) Using the Gettysburg Address as a model, write a miniature formal essay for some contemporary occasion: the razing of a landmark in your city, the retirement of a favorite professor, the dedication of a new library or hospital, announcement of the school's probation list for this semester.

6) Write a full-length formal essay on some issue of serious concern to you. Assuming you have an intelligent and educated reader waiting for you, probe in depth the pros and cons of the problem you wish to discuss.

6

The Critical Review

A large complex society depends a great deal upon the critical review to direct cultural traffic, to weed out the unworthy and call attention to the laudable. And involved in today's culture explosion, in which we are pursuers of culture whether or no, every one of us depends on the critical review to guide him through the pleasant plethora of books, movies, dramas, concerts, exhibitions, recitals, and performances (of whatever kind) that is so perpetually available.

To write the critical review is indeed to write one of the prevalent forms of prose — a form to be found in the daily newspaper, in the weekly review, in the special journals devoted to cultural diagnoses, as well as in campus tabloids and literary magazines. And to write the critical review is to take an important and responsible part in modern social life. For better or worse, the critical review has wide influence: many readers (too many perhaps) will take the review as gospel and will act accordingly.

A responsible reviewer must therefore pay especial attention to the form of his review, for in giving thought to the form he will be led to write more carefully, more convincingly, and it is to be hoped — more wisely.

The Critical Review as a Form

Several things a critical review is *not.* First of all, a critical review *is not simply a summary or report:* it is not a book report, a movie report, a concert report. Reports and summaries simply present a factual, non-evaluative synopsis or contents-listing of a work of art or a performance, while a critical review has something to say about the success or failure, the good or bad of the subject under consideration.

And second, a critical review *is not a work of literary criticism.* A critical review may be based upon values discussed in a critical essay, but while literary criticism deals more with an explanation or interpretation of a work, the review concerns itself with the "good or bad."

Literary criticism — and critical essays dealing with other media — tell us what is and what is not present in a work, pointing out its form, its tradition, its technical achievements — and many times illuminating its very meaning. Literary criticism is primarily concerned with identification, in the broadest sense of the word. A critical review, however, assuming identification, tries to come to a sane and practical evaluation — and guide the reader to some particular action: read or not read the book, watch or not watch the show, attend or not attend the "happening."

A good critical review (and one must realize that a lot of bad ones are published) is marked primarily by clear and definite criteria, and by a sense of moderation and reasonableness.

It is almost impossible to discuss the merits and weaknesses of anything unless one has *a definite set of values* by which to measure. Criticism is based upon values — and a good critical review presents value judgments in a convincing way. A review based on other than clear and discernible values will be ambiguous, evasive, and meaningless. Even if one is a wholehearted relativist as far as the universe is concerned, when it comes to writing a critical review relativism should be set aside. In a critical review, one must simply take one's stand — and take it on the basis of predetermined values, predetermined criteria of judgment. A good review doesn't stammer around, trying to make up its mind.

The criteria involved in the critical review may be either (1) impersonal, objective, even scientific, or (2) personal and subjective. Sometimes the critical criteria are those to which many educated people subscribe — they are the criteria established by tradition or established within some professional discipline. Based upon such standard or accepted criteria, a review is impersonal and objective. But sometimes the criteria are those in which the reviewer alone believes — and this is his privilege. Good criticism, after all, can help establish new criteria as well as demonstrate the old. One's only obligation, when using subjective and personal criteria, is to spell out his values with a certain amount of clarity or imply them so strongly that they are easy for the reader to formulate. And having once identified them, overtly or by implication, to maintain them consistently within the review.

Some traditional criteria used in judging works of art — including literature — are these: A work of art is good if it is "true to life," if it "communicates," if it is "significant to the times," if it is "well made," and if it "encourages and supports the morals and ethics of the community." You may not agree with these criteria at all. Indeed you may want to reject them altogether and present more meaningful criteria of your own. To do so, you will do well to jot down your criteria in advance — to clarify them for yourself and to have them in verbal form to include in your review. To establish your own criteria, write down a series of statements in the following manner: "I will consider the work I am going to review good if it __________," and then spell out the precise conditions of excellence that you have in mind. A series of three or four criteria statements will usually be adequate. Five would about be the limit. If you try to employ too many criteria in any one review, you may find yourself unable to handle any one criterion adequately and will be unable to prove or illustrate sufficiently to what extent the criteria are satisfied or ignored.

Here for instance would be a useable set of criteria:

> I will consider the book of poetry I am reviewing a good one if the individual poems deal with significant and universally valuable subjects.

I will consider the book of poetry I am reviewing a good one if the individual poems are technically well done as far as rhythm and form are concerned.

I will consider the book of poetry I am reviewing a good one if the poems as a group are held together by some common theme.

I will consider the book of poetry I am reviewing a good one if the book itself is presented in a readable and attractive form.

Though you may not make an actual list of the criteria for inclusion in your review, you may give some indication of what values you have in mind in making your judgment:

> Wholly heartfelt and wholly in hand, these poems are convincing and sympathetic portraits, dramatic and yet philosophically aware. — Charles Philbrick, "Debuts and Encores."*

In that one sentence, the reviewer has pointed out some of the things he thinks a good book of poetry should be.

One method of evaluation, however, is anathema to most educated readers. The good review *avoids irrelevant criteria* — judging a particular work of performance, for instance, by the morality or politics of the creator or performer. To attack the architecture of the Upstate Insurance Building on the grounds that the architect is an alcoholic would be silly at best, irresponsible at worst. Such *ad hominem* arguing — and evaluation — is always to be avoided.

Another attribute of the good review, in addition to its clear criteria, is its *balanced or moderate vision.* Ideally a review contains a balance of praise and censure — though, admittedly, such balance is not always possible. Sometimes a terrible performance is simply a terrible performance and that's all there is to it. But ideally, the critical review does not let itself become entirely an encomium — if it does, it actually moves out of its genre into another. Nor does the critical review let itself become a one-hundred-per-cent jeremiad — if it does, it ceases to be useful and effective.

In general, the balanced vision of a work is best, and the critical review, at *its* best, incorporates moderation into its form. By and large, within the critical review, to validate weaknesses — one must note strengths; to validate strengths — one must note weaknesses. One cannot create the strengths or weaknesses out of whole cloth, of course — but in most cases, as with all things in life, there is both something good and bad to be said. Noting both leads one to wiser conclusions.

As for literary style, *one cannot claim any particular style for the critical review* — the style depends a great deal on the place of publication, the subject being reviewed, the occasion of the criticism. In general, the critical review is more likely to be short and informal than formal and long — simply because of the exigencies of the periodicals in which reviews nowadays appear. But there are notable exceptions — reviews by Edmund Wilson in *The New Yorker,* for instance.

The style may range from dead seriousness to flippancy, from solemnity to wit, from formality to brashness. The good review avoids, however, being so delightful or humorous or petulant or grandiose that the style overwhelms the review — the good reviewer tries not to steal his own show with a heavy stylistic performance.

And as a general practice, the good reviewer does not inject himself into his review, save when he has had some relevant experience or possesses some first-hand information appropriate to the review. If the reviewer has served in the Peace Corps in Africa and is now reviewing a documentary film about Africa, he may indeed refer to personal knowledge. But otherwise, the reviewer does not flaunt his identity.

All in all, the critical review is the most utilitarian of the prevalent prose forms. It, more than other forms, has a definite goal in mind — other forms seek to entertain or instruct, but the critical review goes even further: it seeks to provide the reader with the basis for an immediate decision — to accept or reject, to spend or not to spend time or money. Every aspect of the critical review as a form is devoted to this utilitarian end.

Some of the great names in British and American literary history have been closely associated with the critical review — Samuel Johnson (see for instance his review of Goldsmith's *Traveller* in the *Critical Review*, 1763–64), Edgar Allan Poe (see his famous review of Hawthorne's *Twice-Told Tales*), William Dean Howells, H. L. Mencken, and Edmund Wilson are representative. And in the twentieth century, nearly every prominent literary figure has included the review among his writings: John Updike, Norman Mailer, Robert Lowell, James Dickey all do so. And in fact, nearly any responsible member of any profession is likely to have opportunity — or need — to write the critical review on occasion — professors, physicians, and air force generals review books, plays, events, and objects close to their areas of interest and special knowledge.

With a continuing information explosion in modern life, the critical review becomes more and more important: the busy scholar and scientists, or even the busy pursuer of culture in general, more and more lives in the world of reviews in order to be at least partially informed and aware of the world around him.

How to Write the Critical Review

Before you undertake the actual writing of the critical review, you must make a careful preparation: *examine, experience, and understand the work you are going to evaluate.* If you are not willing to pay close attention to the movie, the recording, the book — then you should not attempt to review it. It would be unethical to review the half-read novel, the slept-through performance. And even if you do observe a work carefully, but do not know what to make of it — you may wish to leave the reviewing to someone else.

A good reviewer knows his own capacities and limitations, and nothing can be more disastrous than the review written by the wrong person. Not that one always has to be an authority; great and significant reviewing is done by educated laymen. Yet one should not be so irresponsible as to attempt to review that for which he has no feeling, no concern, no comprehension. One does not have to be a Tallchief or a Ballanchine to review a ballet, yet one should at least enjoy ballet in general, know something about its techniques and traditions, and have attended a fair number of performances.

Once, however, you feel prepared to make a review then you may proceed in this way:

1) *Write down your first general impression of the work.* Though you finally want, as much as possible, to match specific evidence drawn from the work against specific criteria of judgment, you may start out with over-all reaction and worry about "proving" it later on. Sometimes we know a work is good or bad, but are actually hard pressed to prove it the way a scientist would. You will want to give as detailed a demonstration as possible of how you came to your reaction, but we might as well all candidly admit that a critical review is not a laboratory report: it does involve educated taste and judgment.

2) Having written down your over-all impression, *write down as many details of that over-all judgment as possible.* If your first impression was, "I found the symphony a beautiful and moving piece of music," you will now want to go into detail about what you meant: "I found the symphony a beautiful and moving piece of music — the first movement seems especially novel and lyrical all at once; the third movement seems to be the symphony's greatest achievement." You will go on to note particular passages, or particular use of instruments, and the like.

3) And now, one step further. *Jot down the specific things in the work that led you to your judgments.* "I like the third movement of the symphony because of its intricate but understandable theme, because of its effective use of the string instruments, and because its resolution is adequate without being prolonged."

If you are dealing with literature, as in a book review, you will be able — at this stage — to copy out phrases, sentences, even paragraphs from the work itself in order to provide evidence supporting your conclusions. In the book review, you will want to use a judicious amount of quotation (and in other reviews, too, if the medium of the work in question makes quoting possible) in order to give a certain sense of reality to what you are saying. In quoting from a literary work for review purposes you do not have to worry about the problems of citation as you do in the professional article; you will have already identified the work, and you do not very often have to pin down your quotations to the exact page number. Take care, however, not to quote too much — never let your review become more quotation than commentary. And take care, also, that you do not quote too long a passage at any one time. A few select and choice quotations will serve you better than a whole army of them.

4) And this leads to the observation that in your gathering of judgments and evidence, *you should deal only with the salient characteristics of the work.* Decide what is important in the work, good or bad; what should be truly noted. Don't make the mistake of reviewing insignificant aspects of a work. You may find a ludicrous typographical error — but does it deserve your attention? Or you may find an error in a footnote (a flaw that some nitpicking reviewers from academe love to light upon) — but would it be worthwhile your straightening that particular matter out? Unfortunately, some reviewers amble off the beaten path into the byroads of minutiae simply to display their erudition.

5) Once you have gathered your ammunition, as it were, and have the cannon of your criticism loaded and carefully aimed, you will proceed, most of the time, according to this structural program:

Give a *general identification* of the work you are reviewing. Within the first paragraph of your review, give the name, genre, creator, and any other pertinent information about the subject: "In his new novel, *The Gemini Murder,* Leslie Buchanan has . . . ," or "Ella Fitzgerald's great range of singing style is revealed in her new album, *Whisper Not,* in which she sings love ballads and jazz classics accompanied by seventeen-piece and ten-piece bands conducted by March Piach (Verve V6-4071, $4.79; stereo, $5.79)."

In some instances, the technical identification of the work in question will be given outside the review proper. Reviews in

The New York Times Book Review, for instance, are always headed in this fashion:

> ***Madame Sarah.*** **By Cornelia Otis Skinner. Illustrated. 356 pp. Boston: Houghton Mifflin Company. $6.95.**

In such cases, you may plunge in without telling your reader who, what, when, where, and why — but at all other times, you will have to provide the identification within the text proper — within the very first paragraph.

6) After this identification, you will in the first or second paragraph give *a quick evaluation* of the work. You will state in a sentence or two your over-all opinion of it. In general, this work is good. In general, this work is bad. In general, this work will appeal only to children. In general, this work represents a great literary triumph. In the critical review, you should not play guessing games with your reader, and you should not insist that he wait until the end of the review to find out what your judgment is. Though you will go on to give the details of your judgment, you should give your opinion — your thesis as it were — early in your writing.

Immediate evaluations, elaborated upon as the reviews proceed, are given in these opening paragraphs from recent items published in the *Saturday Review:*

> ***The New Industrial State,*** **by John Kenneth Galbraith. (Houghton-Mifflin. 427 pp. $6.95).**
>
> For some years John Kenneth Galbraith has been poking, prodding, and irritating America toward a measure of understanding of its economic life. His sardonic *Affluent Society* devastated one section of sanctified generalizations. This time he has tackled the more serious task of laying out an economic theory corresponding to its major facts. The book is long overdue. *The New Industrial State* will make economic history. — Adolf A. Berle, "Analyzing the Corporate-Complex."*

* From *Saturday Review,* June 24, 1967. Reprinted by permission of *Saturday Review.*

***Washington, D.C.*, by Gore Vidal (Little Brown, 377 pp. $6.95).**

Gore Vidal's new novel starts with a rainstorm that promises literary lightning. Instead, Mr. Vidal has produced a squall that spends itself on a sea of sex, self-destruction, and cynicism, and ends by dismissing the human race as "no more than bacteria upon a luminous slide." His characters all but drown themselves in cliches and predictable situations, which make his work neither heroic, tragic, nor humorous — just tired and threadbare. Although *Washington, D.C.* is saved from total bankruptcy by occasional flashes of fine prose, the book leaves a lingering frustration because Mr. Vidal's diagnosis of our democratic dilemma is too pat and all surface, as the plot and characters clearly indicate. — Jeffrey St. John, "Brutus on Capitol Hill."*

7) On many occasions, you will give — early in the review — *necessary background information* in order to orient your reader to the terms and conditions of your criticism. Not every review takes time out to present a context, but when the reviewer is not confined to a few hundred words he often will give historical background or ideological background or biographical background to make the work he is discussing more meaningful and more significant for his reader. If the review is of a new piece of sculpture, the reviewer may say something about the state of sculpture today in America and about the particular category of sculpture in question. If the review is an author's seventh novel, some word about the author's previous novels may be appropriate. Or if the review is of a biography of Handel, something may be said about the eighteenth century, about English musical society in that time — or, in another direction, something may be said about the current writing of biography, or how this particular work compares with previous biographies of Handel.

The following example demonstrates a reviewer's need to "set the stage" for his criticism of a particular work:

***Self and Society: Social Change and Individual Development.* By Nevitt Sanford. Atherton. $8.95.**

Nevitt Sanford is a distinguished American psychologist whose career has been unusually rich and complicated. . . . and now he has gathered . . . past writings and some new observations into a first-rate book whose title, *Self and Society,* indicates its almost daring breadth of concern.

Social scientists essentially sort themselves out into two camps, those who look at the individual's mind and attitudes (whether kept to himself or shared with others) and those whose chief interest is in the "world" people must every day confront, be it the concrete neighborhoods they frequent or the intangible but equally influential climate of values and traditions they call their own enough to pass down over the generations. Although an intellectual division of labor is necessary in any field, the nature of man's life on this planet does not lend itself very well to the process of abstraction, unless the abstractions are worded in a gracefully self-defeating way that ensures theoretical flexibility and protects the truth of our contrariness, our stubborn capacity as diverse human beings to resist the descriptions we so much want to make about ourselves. Concepts like "self" or "society" are thus at once, a necessity, a temptation and very real danger. Somehow we have to gather together our thoughts and our observations, yet in doing so we can confuse our ideas (often pridefully discrete) with the "facts" of existence, hard to convey with *any* words or generalizations. The bitter and childish fights between psychiatrists (and indeed social scientists) over the relative importance of "nature" and "nurture," of the unconscious and the street scene, in the individual's fate, show how much we simply don't know or have yet to clarify — and thus must turn into a cause for intellectual war.

This book will help make for peace . . . — Robert Coles, in *The American Scholar.**

* Reprinted from *The American Scholar,* Volume 36, Number 1, Winter, 1966–67.

In all cases, giving background information or establishing a context for the work to be reviewed is an extension actually of identification. The reviewer must decide to what extent he must make so detailed and educative an identification for his reader.

8) Also, the reviewer many times feels that he must give *a brief summary of a work's contents;* a quick trip through the work; a recreation of the work in miniature. In doing so, the reviewer remains fairly objective — he gives non-evaluative description, reads from the program, or repeats the table of contents. This helps the reader comprehend the dimensions and form of the work being reviewed, and is, of course, presented early in the review — in the first few paragraphs.

Franklin Edgerton, ed. and trans. *The Beginnings of Indian Philosophy.* Cambridge: Harvard University Press, 1965, 362 pp. $8.75.

Those who know the writings of Professor Edgerton will undoubtedly welcome the new volume from his pen as an authoritative pronouncement on early Indian philosophy. . . .

The book consists of six parts. The first part of the book gives a lucid introduction, in about thirty pages, and supplies a necessary background for the materials translated in the later parts. The author has also prefixed an introductory note to each of the later sections regarding the nature and the context of the extracts translated. The translations are further accompanied by elaborate notes on the text and by interpretation of individual passages. A consistent attempt is made throughout to avoid the use of Sanskrit words. A very useful Glossorial Index, which furnishes brief definitions of those Sanskrit words used, is included at the end.

The author knows the difficulties of translation and interpretation . . . — K. L. S. Rao, in *Literature East and West.**

9) And now you are ready to go into details. Having identified the work and given a basic judgment, *you will now want*

* From *Literature East and West,* June, 1966. Reprinted by permission of *Literature East and West* and the author.

to point out the specific weaknesses and the specific strengths. In fact, the body of your critical review will be devoted to this citation of evidence and a guiding of your reader down the road to final opinion.

A good rule to follow is this: if your over-all judgment of the work is favorable, then you will present the weaknesses first and get them out of the way. If, however, the review is generally unfavorable, you will present the good points first — and then go on to the things that led to the unfavorable conclusion. "This novel has many weaknesses. They are . . . But, of course, they are almost unnoticed in the light of the novel's many virtues, which are . . ." Or: "This movie has some exciting and wonderful moments. They are . . . But, unfortunately, the greater part of the movie is a dud. Consider for instance such scenes as . . ."

One can, of course, do just the opposite. In a favorable review, give all the good points first — and then, unobtrusively suggest the bad points. Or vice versa. But to end a favorable review with the bad points has a tendency to negate the previous praise; and to end a bad review with the few good points has a tendency to weaken the criticism in general — to leave a slight hint of apology and compromise.

The only workable alternative to the general rule — con/pro in pro reviews; pro/con in con reviews — is to intermix praise and censure throughout the review. This alternative is frequently used when the reviewer is following the work in its own sequence — that is, he is discussing a book chapter by chapter, and comments on the good and bad of each chapter as he goes along; or he is discussing a drama in some topical order — plot, acting, set, direction — and finds good and bad in each of the parts. Also, by intermixing praise and censure throughout, the reviewer gives less emphasis to either one: though running the risk of a meaningless neutrality, he can, if he is successful, give the impression of great judiciousness on his part.

10) You will, after giving the details of your criticism, *restate your general evaluation,* and then — if possible — *make some sort of recommendation to the reader or come to some sort of significant conclusion.* The recommendation or conclusion may take different forms: Because this movie is a good one, (1) you

should see it. Or (2) it should inspire similar movies. Or (3) it will achieve a certain influence on the political climate of the nation. Or because the movie is bad, (4) we should see in it a dangerous influence in our society. Or (5) it will contribute to the vulgarization of certain subjects. Or (6) we certainly hope the playwright will shift to a more conventional type of drama next time.

The recommendation or conclusion should point out the significance of the work (good or bad) in our society, our culture, our lives. A good review does not just hang upon a work like a price tag — but suggests not only what the worth is, but what the worth implies.

Some typical review "endings" are these: From *The New York Review of Books* — "I hope that, he will carry on, and provide a similar measured, intelligent work on Richardson or Fielding," and "At a time when the behavioral scientists are hot for certainties and computers are unfed in the laboratories of personality research, Anna Freud's book makes it clear that psychoanalysis has little fare to offer the machines. Will it ever? To put it another way, one small child, infinitively complex, can still confound the fortune tellers." From *The New Yorker* — "The post-apocalyptic irresolution of 'Two Views' may well be where European man, after history's extravagant demands, is glad to settle." And from *Saturday Review:* "Projecting this mode of procedure further into the future, it is not impossible that some soloist may commission a work for violin and magnetic tape, say, which he will then proceed to perform without the intervention of an orchestra. Or, by logical extension, without a conductor. Perhaps, there is something to the whole idea after all."

11) One special note about the form of the review: Most reviews deal with single works, of course, but on certain occasions you may wish to attempt some judgment of a set of related works. In such cases you will most likely establish — as a means of unifying your review — some common theme, letting this common theme become your main subject as you proceed to discuss a series of novels, a series of recordings, or a group of paintings.

In a review dealing with several items, you will begin by

identifying your theme—and only then will you proceed in the regular manner of the review (identification, evaluation, and the like) as you discuss one work after another. Your conclusion will, of course, deal with the unifying theme—and frequently your final judgment will be of the theme (its significance, its effect on society, and the like) as well as upon the individual works.

Here are excerpts from a review of three books. In writing the review, Douglas M. Davis identifies and discusses the common theme of "black humor":

> "Black humor" keeps getting blacker. That is the only safe conclusion from the latest products served up by three of its major practitioners — John Hawkes and *The Innocent Party,* a collection of plays; James Purdy and *Eustace Chisholm and the Works,* a novel; and William Burroughs and *The Ticket That Exploded,* another novel. [*First paragraph*]
>
> Let me feed you just a few of the essential goings-on. . . .
>
> As I say, black humor is blacker than ever. I am not sure, however, that it's better than ever. . . .
>
> [*Final paragraph*] The black humorists need to get off dead center esthetically. Rage and disgust alone will not carry a novelist — not through more than one or two books, anyway. — Douglas M. Davis, in *The National Observer.**

12) You will write out your review, of course, in a length determined primarily by the journal, magazine, or newspaper in which the review is likely to appear. If you are writing a review simply for teacher or friends, you may make the review as long as you wish, taking into consideration your audience's depth of interest. But if you are writing for any sort of publication—and that can be anything from a five-minute radio broadcast to a magazine article—you will shape your review to the physical limitations of your medium.

If you are writing a five-minute radio review, you will write some 500 words. If you are writing for *Books Abroad,* you will limit yourself to a quick review of some 100 to 150 words, or whatever limitations the editor prescribes. If you are writing for *Saturday Review*, you may range, it seems, from 500 words to 1000 words. And in some publications, such as *Yale Review* or the *New Yorker*, reviews are sometimes as long as 3000 to 5000 words.

Whatever the length, you will normally use the same basic outline of presentation: identification, quick evaluation, background, weaknesses and strengths (or strengths and weaknesses), restatement of evaluation, and final recommendation or conclusion.

13) And you will, of course, write your review in a style appropriate to your audience and your subject matter. Admittedly, most reviews are written today in a journalistic style — simple, straightforward, deliberate. But there are exceptions. In a long review dealing with some major event, you may have need for a more formal manner; if for instance you were writing about the performances that closed the old Metropolitan House and opened the new, you might write a bit more grandly than otherwise. Or if you are speaking in depth to a highly educated audience, you may allow yourself more linguistic graciousness.

And if you are speaking to an audience especially well-informed in the art form or subject matter of your review, your review may be somewhat more technical. Or in a review for some special, sophisticated "inside" audience, you may inject into your review a certain amount of "entertainment" value — as Dorothy Parker did, delightfully, in her book reviews for *Esquire* magazine.

An example of a fairly popular style in writing a review is seen in this passage from a movie review by Wilfred Sheed:

> A mighty clash of censors has been heard over the movie *Ulysses*, a beating of tin pans and a tooting of penny-whistles, but this must surely be one of their more foolish battles. . . .
>
> As it turns out, the picture is hardly worth the fuss anyway. The first half hour or so is fine, with Stephen Dedalus pacing the sands to the tune of Joyce's finest, and then the men in the coach jogging moodily to the funeral. But after that,

> things come tolerably unstuck. Milo O'Shea makes a pedestrian Leopold Bloom and his night-town fantasies are drawn to peep-show scale. Standing by while Joyce's diabolically gorgeous language is being boiled and watered down to B-movie images is nasty work and calls for a moral. — Wilfred Sheed, "Films."*

The following review — by Russell Kirk in *The Sewanee Review* — comes from the other end of the style spectrum: it is written more conventionally and more learnedly.

> Much the best stylist of our present company, Mr. Bredvold dissects the principal errors of the Enlightenment: the rejection of the theory of natural law; scientism; the sentimental view of human nature; a fashion of "following nature" which is inimical to civilization; a disastrous Utopianism. Contemptuously rejecting the transcendent understanding of man and society which arises from religious knowledge, the *philosophes* exposed modern man to the inner disorder of the soul and the outer disorder of the total state: thus, fancying themselves liberators, they enslaved the world to appetite and unchecked power. — Russell Kirk, "Ideologues' Folly."†

All in all, your style can vary from the more formal manner of a *Yale Review* to the standard journalistic manner of the *Saturday Review* to the cute and breezy way of *Time Magazine* to the almost anonymous, scholarly-oriented language found in the back of many professional journals.

When you have finished writing your review, put it aside for a day. If possible, reread the book, re-view the movie, listen once again to the music. You may have second thoughts. And you may want to check out your criticisms once again, to make sure that in trying to serve an audience by guiding them toward or diverting them from some particular experience, you have always written with honesty, sincerity, and good taste.

* Reprinted from *Esquire*, July, 1967.

† From *The Sewanee Review*, Volume LXXI, Number 2, Spring, 1963. Copyright by the University of the South. Reprinted by permission of *The Sewanee Review* and the author.

An Exemplary Critical Review

Kids Without a Country

The Uncommitted:
Alienated Youth in American Society
by Kenneth Keniston
Harcourt, Brace & World, 495 pp., $8.50

EDGAR Z. FRIEDENBERG

In this excellent, original, and lucid work, Kenneth Keniston has undertaken to analyze and explain a phenomenon that has certainly come to engross Americans as never before. *The Uncommitted* is a study in depth by a gifted and imaginative psychologist of the processes that lead many of our brightest youth to despise and reject the society in which they have grown up and which has afforded them its best opportunities and advantages. He has studied this problem in the following way:

> From a large group of undergraduate men, twelve were identified by psychological tests as extremely alienated. These were selected for special study, along with another group of twelve who were extremely non-alienated, and a third "control group" of students who were not extreme either way. All were asked to take part in a three-year study of their personal development.
>
> For this study, all of the students wrote a lengthy autobiography and a statement of their basic values and "philosophy of life." All took the Thematic Apperception Test (T.A.T.), which consists of twenty cards, each showing an ambiguous picture, for each of which the research subjects are asked to make up a story. All the students also took part in a wide variety of psychological experiments, ranging

from the systematic observations of five-man groups to studies of self-image, from investigations of moral values to research into personal identity. And all were repeatedly interviewed about matters autobiographical, philosophical, and experimental. For three academic years, most gave about two hours a week to the research.

The research reported in *The Uncommitted,* then, is wholly psychological. But the problem of alienation is as much social as psychological, as Keniston emphasizes both explicitly and in the very structure of his book: It is divided into two sections, "Alienated Youth" and "Alienating Society." The purpose of this division is clearly to emphasize that society and the individual contribute dialectically to the individual's alienation. Any excessive stress on psychological factors, or underemphasis on society's contribution, in principle contributes to the bias which Keniston states in his first chapter he is most anxious to avoid:

> The most powerful analyses of our society, like our most profound understandings of human nature, are too often taken as apologies for the status quo. We commonly interpret them to mean that our society is basically sound and that those who cannot reconcile themselves to it would profit more from psychotherapy than from social reform. I think we already hear enough from the pulpits of Academia as well as the megaphones of the mass media about the oppotunities, challenges, productivity, material standards, and achievements of our society. We attend too superficially to the human price we pay for these achievements, rarely entertaining the thought that our society's accomplishments may have outrun its purposes, leaving us with outlived and outworn values. These themes, rather than the virtues of American society, are those I have stressed here.

But despite this *caveat* to the general, Keniston remains psychoanalytic in all particulars. The picture of personality structure underlying alienation in upper-middle-class youth that emerges is convincing and relevant. Any doubts one may have about generalizing from a twelve-man sample dissolve as soon as one reads Keniston's construction of how these young men came to be what and who they are; it is *right,* as obviously as those dinosaurs at a World's Fair Sinclair Pavilion are *right;* what the painstaking techniques of science create proves to be, happily, just what the imagination requires. To summarize is inevitably to do injustice to the clarity and richness of Keniston's discussion. What the uncommitted have in common, etiologically, is the experience of having been reared in families in which the father, though often celebrated in the great society, has withdrawn from the demands of family life and particularly from those of his wife; in which the wife and mother has responded by becoming seductive and treacherous in her urgent need to extract at least minimal attention and emotional support from her husband and sons. As boys, these alienated subjects respond by hating and mistrusting the father for his weakness, and fearing the mother for her ability to get them on her side and use them against the father whose wretchedness brings them to despair. There is no one they can trust. Consequently:

> The alienated consciously and unconsciously see adulthood in our society as asking a price that they are unable and unwilling to pay. Unconsciously, adulthood involves relinquishing for good the fantasy of infantile fusion; consciously, it involves "selling out," abandoning their dreams and visions, committing themselves to people, institutions, and causes which they see as making destructive claims on them. Adulthood means accepting an adult self-definition which entails limitation of awareness, openness, and genuineness; it involves materialism, boring work, being controlled by the demands of others.

This is a pivotal passage in Keniston's argument, and he is quick to guard against its misuse. His methodology has obliged him to speak in psychoanalytic terms; and he immediately cautions us that:

> The very existence of reluctance . . . should make us ask whether the rejection of adulthood may not be related to the demands of adulthood itself. We must entertain once again the possibility that the alienated are responding not only to their own psychic predispositions but to the facts of adult life in America.

The second half of *The Uncommitted* deals with those facts as Keniston interprets them. It is very good in its way, clear and telling; but it is far less authoritative than the first half. Here, Keniston is not dealing at all with his own data or even with primary sources; what he gives us is an extended essay on American civilization and its discontents rather in the manner of Daniel Boorstin or David Riesman. What he is trying to do in this essay, is to explain what it is in the way our society works, that makes it particularly hard on "The Uncommitted."

His psychological training permits him, in doing this, to make use of an analytic tool seldom employed in studying the workings of society, but admirably suited to his purpose. The very first name in Keniston's Acknowledgements is that of the late Henry A. Murray. It is Murray, of course, who developed the T.A.T. referred to earlier as a central instrument in Keniston's study. But, more than that, Murray also developed the intellectual structure on which *The Uncommitted* is based. This is the idea that the interaction between an individual and his environment may be most clearly categorized and described if the individual's *needs* are thought of as interlocking with a corresponding set of what Murray calls "environmental press." The same terms are used in describing both needs and "press"; and adjustment is most comfortable in a situation in which they are complementary rather than similar. A man with a strong need for abasement, for example, will relish a situation that presses to dominate him, while one in which he was treated with respect would make him more nervous. The needs-press formulation is not, of course, a psychological theory; it is merely a kind of cartographic device. Keniston does not make formal use of Murray's categories and terminology; but he follows him in treating society as a set of *demands* that impinge on its members, who then respond according to their own needs.

This approach helps Keniston clarify, when he discusses "Alienating Society," what it is specifically about the society that bugs alienated youth. Parts of this discussion are really brilliantly helpful. I like especially his chapter on "The Dictatorship of the Ego," in which he shows how the development of the rational, highly cognitive "technological ego" is cultivated by our society at the expense of feeling and moral sensitivity. His kind of alienated youth, who are encumbered by excessive feeling and almost morbid moral sensitivity, are thereby forced into an anti-intellectual posture (non-alienated, or Gung-Ho, types would say "posture") that deprives them of the use of their superior intellectual skills, which they might have deployed on behalf of the values they cherish — thus diminishing further their chance and their inclination to commit themselves to any kind of social action.

But society is more than just the environment; it is an organism with structure and functions, if not purposes, of its own. By treating it as if it were a set of environmental press, Keniston's discussion of society overstresses its effect on how it makes people feel about it and about themselves. Society, however, consists of far more than our emotional response to it: institutions, roles, networks of communication, hierarchies, all of which affect, not only our feelings, but our expectations, and our opportunities and inclinations to do something about our feelings. He does a fine job of showing what it is in our society that makes it just the sort to which uncommitted youths are most poorly adapted, and least likely to commit themselves; and he conscientiously affirms and reaffirms that this is as much society's fault as theirs. But his mode of analysis prevents him from taking account of how *actual* changes in our social situation may affect the behavior of the uncommitted, not by altering their character or feelings but by making them an appropriate basis for social action. He attributes to alienated youth a disaffection so deep-seated and chronic as to disable them politically:

> Strong in opposition, these young men are weak in affirmation; unable to articulate or even to know what they stand for, they have little sense of self to stand on. . . But rebels without a cause can only stand against, not for; and even their opposition is diffuse and unspecific. The price they pay for this opposition, a price exacted by all societies (which must refuse sanctioned identity to their opponents), is inner confusion, disunity, and fragmentation. For this reason, if for no other, it is far easier psychologically to be revolutionary with a program than an alienated youth with only a vague set of rejections.

But since this was written, our rebels without a cause have become revolutionaries — though still mostly without a program; they are more nearly anarchists than ideologues. What has changed is not the character structure of the Uncommitted — Keniston's portrayal of one of these, Inburn, and his confrères at Berkeley still basically resembles the young men of the Free Speech Movement and the Vietnam Day Committee, though the Berkeley style and the Harvard style remain very different — but the society. Society was never as monolithic as Keniston rather smugly states; but pluralistic. His statement that "all societies . . . must refuse sanctioned identity to their opponents" is quite false. The fact is that most functioning societies provide and institutionalize such identity, as we do for conscientious objectors, and by legal recognition of the right to dissent. And, so far, these norms have held up even under considerable pressure. The Uncommitted have been learning how to use them. People, even young people, always have more freedom than they dare to use; but lately, dissenting youth has been shifting into overdrive and risking jail.

Perhaps the most important factor in crystalizing alienated youth into social activists is the simple fact that our society has become morally insufferable. During the period when *The Uncommitted* was in preparation, the murder of the President and of his putative assassin spread a sense of horror among all of us. The young have seen their country commit, deny, and later boast of the very actions it has most harshly condemned and sought to punish in others: in Cuba, Vietnam, and Santo Domingo. American leadership, throughout this time, has behaved with peculiar duplicity and been caught out with disturbing frequency. The CIA has conspired to overthrow governments in every part of the world by force and violence. An eminent historian who ought, presumably, to have been governed by a historian's regard for fact in a matter of historical importance, helped conceal the nature of its operation by grossly understating to *The New York Times* the size of the Bay of Pigs invasion force. Confronted with this discrepancy a few weeks ago, Mr. Schlesinger is quoted as responding: "Did I say that? Well, I was lying — that was the cover story." Meanwhile, my fellow sociologists, enthralled by the first six-million-dollar contract sociology had ever seen, went enthusiastically to work for the Army gathering information in various countries to be used in counter-insurgency. They called this "Project Camelot" because "It connotes the right sort of things — development of a stable society with peace and justice for all"*; "It never seemed to occur to its personnel," Professor Horowitz reports, "to inquire into the desirability of successful revolution. . . . Furthermore, they seem not to have thought about inquiring into the role of the United States in these countries. . . . The propriety of the Army to define and delimit all questions, which Camelot should have had a right to examine, was never placed in doubt."

Things have changed. When Keniston's exemplary, and archly pseudonymous, Inburn was growing up to be alienated, people were still being shocked about Charles Van Doren's betrayal of the role and dignity of the Professor. One result of this deterioration — and particularly, I should think, of the corruption of academic life by its devotion to our National Purpose — must surely have been to broaden the base of protest among the young, who have

* Irving Louis Horowitz, "The Life and Death of Project Camelot" *Transaction* 3, 1, Nov./Dec. 1965.

a right to expect universities to be devoted to their education. This reduces the relevance of any attempt to explain their disaffection in psychodynamic terms, because people no longer need have very much in common personally to find our present society repugnant enough to arouse protest. Uncommitted youth may have been the first to wither in a social climate in which they perceived that "adulthood means accepting an adult self-definition which entails limitation of awareness, openness, and genuineness; it involves materialism, boring work, being controlled by the demands of others." But when Adlai Stevenson dropped dead in a London street, it was clear that he was the victim of a plague — an epidemic, not an idiosyncratic disorder. Men cannot go on living as we live, here in Finkistan, whether they would or not. The great irony of Kenneth Keniston's work is that, in undertaking to explain why some of the young refuse to try, he did not find it more curious that so many more manage to accept our lethal way of life.

An Analysis

1) Although the book being discussed in this critical review is identified outside the review itself, to what extent does Friedenberg re-identify his subject in his text?
2) Why does Friedenberg give the author's full name in the last sentence of the review? Throughout the review he simply refers to "Keniston," but at the end he says "Kenneth Keniston."
3) For what sort of reader is Friedenberg writing? How can you tell? Look especially at vocabulary, allusions, and references.
4) How does Friedenberg proceed through the book — does he follow the book itself, going right down through the table of contents? Or does he jump around here and there, following some special kind of organization and order?
5) Since this is a well-written review it is not simply a summary of contents. But can you, nevertheless, abstract from the review a fairly reasonable report of what the book actually contains? Ignoring all value and judgment statements, outline briefly the book's structure and contents.

6) Though the summary of the reviewer's position is given immediately in the review—"In this excellent, original, and lucid work"—does Friedenberg make any real criticisms of the book? What are they? At what point in the review does he present them?

7) And *how* does Friedenberg present his criticisms? Note that in addition to explicit statements of disagreement on his part, Friedenberg also throws in a comment like "Keniston rather smugly states . . ." To what extent does the reviewer use such words as "smugly," and how effective are they? Do they hurt or help the review?

8) Is the final sentence of the review a genuine criticism?

9) Can you identify some of the criteria Friedenberg is using in this review? On what basis does he praise or censure the book? Make a list of the "good things" you think Friedenberg would want in a book. Make a list of the "bad things" he wouldn't want.

10) Friedenberg takes his role as reviewer seriously enough to try to place *The Uncommitted* in the context of contemporary concerns. In what part of the review does he make his greatest effort to go beyond the book itself and present a context?

11) Can you make any observations about Friedenberg's use of quotations from the book he is reviewing? Actually his quotations are rather long, especially the first and second ones. Do you think they are too long? Or do you think it was necessary that the quotations be ample?

12) A good review makes as much specific reference to the work being reviewed as possible. In addition to the specific quotations, in what other ways does Friedenberg bring us to the book so that we feel he is not just making up his evidence?

13) Since a review is primarily for immediate use, it can be more topical and more ephemeral in its allusions and references. Cite in this review some names, words, expressions that are meaningful now, but may not necessarily be meaningful five or ten years from now.

14) How many times does Friedenberg use the first person pronoun?
15) Just how much does Friedenberg get into the review himself — how much of his own personality appears? Do you think it is too much? Or does he strike just about the right tone of involvement with his subject?

Assignments

1) Identify the criteria, stated or implied, in the front-page review in a recent issue of *The New York Times Book Review.* Are any of the criteria unacceptable? Are the judgments in the review consistent with the stated criteria?
2) After seeing a movie that you have especially liked, look up a review of it in *Time, Holiday,* the *New York Times, Saturday Review,* or your local newspaper. Do you agree with the review? If not, why not? Do you feel the review has erred in the use of criteria or in the use of evidence?
3) Compare two reviews of the same book — say a review form *Atlantic* or *Harper's* with one from *The American Scholar* or *Western Humanities Review.* How do you account for the difference?
4) Write a review of a book you have recently read. Write first a 250-word review. Then write a longer review, say of about 1000 words.
5) Write a 1000-word review of a television comedy show. Prepare for the review by establishing in advance some of the specific things you will be looking for, by establishing your criteria, and by watching some other television comedy show for the sake of comparison.
6) Write a review of a building, a painting, or a piece of music. First, find one of these that you dislike; write a negative review — and yet at the same time a fair and just review. Second, find one of the subjects — building, painting, musical composition — that you like very much; write a favorable review — and yet at the same time avoid meaningless praise and panegyrics.

A Note on Publishing

The realities of publishing are such that you may not feel committed enough to your writing to pursue the matter. (It takes a certain amount of persistence and audacity to get into print.) But even if the present state of your art is inauspicious, it may not always be so. With experience you will become a more confident and articulate writer. And the odds are not so great that any reasonably competent writer cannot sooner or later publish. But whether you are writing for publication or not, your object should always be to write as professionally as you can. Make every writing job — notes, letters, minutes, reports, research papers, essay exams, the articles and essays and reviews you write for English Composition — an occasion for practicing and perfecting your art. With that sort of attitude you will achieve a reputation with all who read your prose as being that most rare and envied person, "a good writer"; and you may, if you follow more or less the procedures outlined here, become a publishing writer as well.

Writing for publication is not the same as writing to please your instructor or yourself. The criteria an editor applies to your work are likely to be quite different. He is looking for special qualities — relevance and novelty, flash and sophistication, smoothness and succinctness. Since he reads infinitely more manuscripts than he could ever use, an editor will reject yours for the slightest of reasons. Certainly he will not be the indulgent and encouraging critic you have been accustomed to find in your instructor. So you will have to begin taking your writing more seriously if you expect to publish. If you don't, who will?

Surveying the Field

Find out which journals and magazines publish the forms you write best. For example, if you are most at home in the personal essay, look at *Atlantic Monthly, Blackwoods, Harper's, Holiday, The New Yorker, Saturday Review,* etc. Notice which lengths, subjects, styles editors seem to favor. Find out for yourself the kind of personal essay being published these days. Don't aim too high at first; get published anywhere; begin building up a list of credits; then you will be assured of a more attentive reading by editors who see your work.

Writing for a Particular Audience

You have probably already noticed that magazines and journals have distinct preferences about what they print. Your chances of getting published by an editor are much greater if you have written something or can write something that appeals to his tastes. "Slanting" what you write, as it is sometimes called, is not difficult. Writers have always adapted their material to a particular audience. And an editor's preferences are generally based on what he believes to be those of his readers. The kind of material that would interest one editor would probably be of interest to others whose publications were in a similar class. Certainly it would be a waste of time to send your personal essay to a magazine that has never been known to print one, or to a journal that publishes only scholarly articles and an occasional formal essay. Read the publication to see if there is any statement made about editorial policy or submitting manuscripts. Quite often they will request that you follow a particular style sheet, or ask for two copies of any material, or say that they do not read unsolicited manuscripts and must be queried first.

The Manuscript

Naturally all that has been said about the readable manuscript applies here. A manuscript of professional quality is correct, neat, and conventional. Anything less will not receive a very favorable reading and will likely be summarily returned. Right or wrong, it's that old matter of first appearances again.

The Cover Letter

A very brief letter should accompany your submission. It need say no more than, in effect, "here is my manuscript." It should not try to explain or justify what you have written, but may contain information about yourself and your publishing record which might induce the editor to give the material a more careful reading. Be brief, however — one page at the most — or you will do more harm than good.

Mailing the Manuscript

Address the editor by name if you know it (and you can usually find out by consulting the current issue of *Literary Market Place*) or simply "The Editor" if you do not. Send the manuscript first class if it is light or by the special rate if it is heavier. Shorter manuscripts can be folded once in a 5″ x 7″ envelope or folded as a letter in a standard business-size envelope; longer manuscripts should be mailed flat in a 9″ x 12″ envelope, with perhaps a piece of cardboard enclosed to stiffen and protect it. Be sure to enclose a self-addressed, stamped envelope. And always keep a copy of your work. Above all, keep your manuscripts in circulation; if one is rejected by an editor, send it immediately to the next most likely place.

Keep Writing

The true professional stays at his typewriter. If what you have written isn't accepted, what you write next will be better — and may be published.

INDEX TO AUTHORS